Ethel Carnie Holdsworth

Collected Poems

The Ethel Carnie Holdsworth Series

General Editor: Nicola Wilson

Patricia E. Johnson is Professor Emerita of English and Humanities at Penn State University. She has published two articles on Ethel Carnie, one on her poetry (Victorian Poetry, vol. 43.3, 2005) and one on her fairy tales (Marvels & Tales, vol. 30.2, 2016). She is also the author of *Hidden Hands: Working-Class Women and Victorian Social Problem Fiction* (Ohio UP, 2001) as well as articles on the novels of Charlotte Bronte, Elizabeth Gaskell, Margaret Oliphant, Charles Dickens, and Pat Barker.

Nicola Wilson is Associate Professor in Book and Publishing Studies and Co-director of the Centre for Book Cultures & Publishing at the University of Reading. She is the author of *Home in British Working-Class Fiction* (Ashgate, 2015) and has published on working-class writing in *Key Words; The Oxford History of the Novel in English, vol. 7* (2015); and *A History of British Working Class Literature* (2016). In 2011 she introduced and edited Ethel Carnie Holdsworth's 1925 novel, *This Slavery* (Trent).

Ethel Carnie Holdsworth

Collected Poems

Rhymes from the Factory
(with additions)

Songs of a Factory Girl

Voices of Womanhood

With an Introduction by Patricia E. Johnson

Kennedy & Boyd

2020

Kennedy & Boyd
an imprint of
Zeticula Ltd
Unit 13,
196 Rose Street,
Edinburgh,
EH2 4AT

http://www.kennedyandboyd.co.uk
admin@kennedyandboyd.co.uk

Rhymes from the Factory first published in 1907 by R. Denham,
   Blackburn. Second edition, with additions, first published in
   1908
Songs of a Factory Girl first published in 1911 by Headley
   Brothers, London.
Voices of Womanhood first published in 1914 by Headley Brothers,
   London
This edition Copyright © Zeticula Ltd 2020
First published in this edition 2020

Note on the text:
The copy-text for *Rhymes* is the Denham Second edition.
The copy-text for *Songs* and *Voices* is Headley Brothers text. The
   text of the current edition, set in Bookman, follows that of the
   original text as closely as possible, retaining older forms of
   English usage and grammar.
Ethel Carnie Holdsworth published under her maiden name (Ethel
   Carnie) and with various versions of her married name.

Front cover image: Ethel Carnie Holdsworth.
Reproduced with kind permission from Helen Brown.

ISBN 978-1-84921-212-0

CONTENTS

Ethel Carnie.

Introduction

The rediscovery of Ethel Carnie's writings has taken decades, and scholars and readers are just beginning to appreciate the scope of her achievements. Carnie is recognized as the first working-class woman novelist in the UK and the first to sustain a long and varied writing career. Her literary output is impressive: she published three books of poetry, four books of original fairy tales, and eleven novels as well as numerous poems, short stories, and journalistic pieces in newspapers and magazines. She was also a political activist, engaged in the union and women's suffrage movements. Her political beliefs were independent and prescient: she was an ardent pacifist and internationalist and, in 1924, cofounded the National Union for Combating Fascism, the first anti-fascist organisation in the UK.

This volume republishes Carnie's three books of poetry. Poetry was the first literary genre that she wrote in, and these two books illustrate her experiment with literary form as a way to express the realities of working-class life, especially for women. Her final book of poems, *Voices of Womanhood*, in particular, demonstrates the strength of her radical working-class and feminist vision.

The Biographical Context

The daughter of two cotton mill workers, Ethel Carnie was raised in Lancashire, born in Oswaldtwistle in 1886 and living in nearby East Harwood afterward. Her father was a member of the Social Democratic Federation, the UK's first Marxist political party, and often took his daughter to meetings with him. Her full-time education consisted of five years at the Nonconformist British School. Then, as was typical of working-class children of the time period, at the age of 11 she began half-time work at Delph Road factory as a reacher and at age 13 full-time work as a winder at St. Lawrence mill. She continued full-time factory work until 1909.[1]

With her girlhood and young womanhood spent in a factory, Carnie wrote about working-class life from personal experience. In a series of editorials published in 1909 in Woman Worker, she provided a stinging indictment of the factory system:

> Factory life has crushed the childhood, youth, maturity of millions of men and women. It has ruined the health of those who would have been comparatively strong but for the unremitted toil and the evil atmosphere.[2]

In her essay, "We Who Work," she powerfully describes her personal reaction to factory life:

. . . I hated the narrow, monotonous, long day . . . the torture of the turning wheels, the whirling straps, the roar and rattle of the machinery when I have come to my place sick with cold, or tired with running lest I should be late.[3]

She survived her years of factory work with spirit intact through reading and, then, writing. Like many of her peers, she was an autodidact who would work ten hours a day in the mill and then stay up half the night reading. At the mill, she describes seeing fellow workers with books in their pockets. Like her, they smuggled them in to read them propped against their looms, and, thus, she says, "Between the breaking of the threads and the threading of the shuttle, we thieve back a little of the time that they [the factory owners] are thieving from us."[4]

In her teenage years, she began publishing poems in newspapers such as *The Blackburn Mail* and attracted the attention of W. H. Burnett, editor of the *Blackburn Standard and Express* and president of the Blackburn Authors' Association. He helped her to publish her first book of poetry, *Rhymes from the Factory*, in 1907. When *Rhymes* quickly sold out its first printing of 500 copies, a second edition was published in 1908. Carnie dedicated both this book and her third book of poems, *Voices of Womanhood*, to Burnett, "my first literary friend."

Rhymes from the Factory, is, primarily, a celebration of Carnie's imaginative escape from her workplace. In the Preface, she writes,

'Twas in this period [when she was working full-time as a winder] that I wrote "The Bookworm," which seems to have attracted the most attention of any of my writings. It was really composed whilst working at my frame. I think it is no exaggeration to say that all my poems came into my head at the mill.[5]

As her biographer Roger Smalley states, she was "diffident" about her writing abilities[6]; she stated, "I trust my critics will be kindly and charitable, and will bear in mind the circumstances of my education, which hardly favours the writing of polished verse."[7] Written when she was a teenager, Rhymes shows a poet learning her craft. She is careful to cite her reading as evidence of the study she has devoted to literature and the mainstream British poetic tradition. Her poems name, for example, Thomas Carlyle, John Keats, and Robert Burns. She also demonstrates her familiarity with classical antiquity, writing poems entitled "Daphne" and "The Last Days of Pompeii." In general, these early poems are written in accepted Victorian poetic diction with genteel thoughts about such topics as "Friendship" and "Youth, Hope and Love."

Rhymes' central theme is the ideal world of literature as a place where a reader can be freed of class distinctions and material realities. "The Bookworm," the volume's first poem, states:

I own no grand baronial hall,
No pastures rich in waving corn;
Leave unto me my love for books,
And wealth and rank I laugh to scorn. . .

For I am heir to an estate
That Fortune cannot take from me,
The treasure-rooms of Intellect,
With gates ajar eternally.

Rhymes shows the working-class factory poet roaming the world in her imagination, traveling from Italy to the Indies. Despite the fact that she composed these poems at her loom, they do not reveal a great deal about working-class life or, for the most part, express a political viewpoint. Poems, such as "The Rich and the Poor" and "The God of Gold," do state "our system's wrong," but they do not go on to suggest any solution to the problem of class inequality.

After the publication of *Rhymes from the Factory*, Carnie's life changed as she gained recognition as a remarkable factory girl poet. This change enabled her to leave full-time factory work, an event that she described as like an escape from a cage.[8] (It should be noted, however, that, because her income from writing was small and irregular, she worked on and off in the factory until 1923). The transforming event was her meeting with Robert Blatchford, editor of *The Clarion*. Intrigued by *Rhymes*, Blatchford decided to see this remarkable factory girl for himself. He visited her in Great Harwood, which he described as a typically oppressive Lancashire mill town, "a monstrous agglomeration of ugly factories, of ugly gasometers, of ugly houses." Carnie herself he approved of; in his article entitled "A Lancashire Fairy," he describes her as small, plain, modest, and a little shy and bestows on her the accolade of being "a real lady in the best sense of that ill-used word."[9] The factory fined Carnie for the work hours she missed for her visit with Blatchford.

In 1909, Blatchford hired the twenty-two year old Ethel Carnie to write for his publication *Woman Worker*, and she moved to London. What happened during the eight months of her employment there is unclear, but her biographer Roger Smalley thinks Carnie's views on labour and women's position proved too radical for Blatchford. Perhaps the political modesty of the poems in *Rhymes from the Factory* led Blatchford to misunderstand her character. At the end of the eight months, Blatchford removed her from her full-time position, although she still published occasional poems and journalistic pieces for him.

The years leading up to the publication of Ethel Carnie's second book of poetry, *Songs of a Factory Girl* (1911), are not well-documented. It appears she returned to factory work in Great Harwood while continuing to write. In the 1911 census, she lists her occupations as "cotton winder and journalist." The years between 1911 and the publication of her third and final book of poetry, *Voices of Womanhood*, in 1914 are better documented, showing Carnie's wide variety of activities. During this period, she supported herself both by writing and, as was typical of many working-class women, a variety of other jobs, including work in the draper's shop her mother had taken and selling ribbons at the Blackburn market. She attended night classes at Owens College in Manchester and also travelled to London regularly to teach at Bebel House Women's College and Socialist Education Centre where she founded the Rebel Pen Club of Working Women to encourage other working-class women to write and publish. She also left the UK for the first and only time to visit Germany to write a series of travel essays.

Her published writings during this period are varied and remarkable, revealing that this was a period of intense creativity for her. In addition to working on her final book of poems, she began work to write in other genres. She published four volumes of original fairy tales, three of them in the popular Books for the Bairns series, founded by W. T. Stead in order to create inexpensive books for working-class children. Her fourth volume of fairy tales, *The Lamp Girl and Other Stories*, published separately by Headley Brothers in 1914, contains a number of powerful tales that are marked by her socialist feminist vision and are an important, though overlooked, contribution to this genre. She began to work in the genre she would devote most of her creative energy to for the next two decades, publishing her first novel, *Miss Nobody*, in 1913. Her final book of poems, *Voices of Womanhood*, is the last achievement of this fertile period.

The Working-Class Literary Context

As a novelist, Carnie is recognized as a pioneer. Her poetry should also be recognized as a unique achievement. Her three books of poetry reveal a steady advance in skill and in the growth of a strong, distinctive working-class vision that is broadly communal, incorporating both socialist and feminist themes. In creating her vision, Carnie draws together two streams of nineteenth-century working-class poetry—that of Chartism and of working-class women.

Poetry was a very popular genre with working-class readers and writers. Many newspapers, such as the Chartist *Northern Star*, featured poetry columns that received hundreds of submissions a week. At working-class meetings, original songs and ballads were sung. Chartist poets, such as Ernest Jones and Thomas Cooper, found enthusiastic audiences. Their poetry used a collective voice to call for action against an oppressive system and for radical economic and societal change. It is important to note, however, that Chartist authors were primarily male and, in fact, Chartist politics banned women from active engagement. The collective voice and revolutionary fervor of Chartist poetry can be seen in Carnie's poetry but not its emphasis on male power and female subservience.

In addition, Carnie shares elements with earlier working-class women poets, such as Ellen Johnston (1835-1873) and Fanny Forrester (1852-89). Like them, she first published her poetry in regional and working-class newspapers and, through that activity, found a mentor who helped her to publish her first volume. For example, Ellen Johnston, also a famous factory girl poet, found a mentor in Alexander Campbell, editor of the *Penny Post*, who solicited subscriptions in his paper to support the publication of Johnston's collected poems.[10] While Carnie's general background and education are similar to Johnston's, her poetry is very different. Johnston's poetry often dramatizes her own life, focusing on personal struggles and betrayals. Carnie, however, seldom writes about herself personally, instead using either a collective voice or the voice of a particular fictional working-class woman that she has created. Carnie does address some of the topics found as such poets as the Scots Janet Hamilton (1795-1873); these include the death of poor children, sympathetic portrayals of fallen women, and critiques of domestic violence. However, there are notable differences between these earlier poets and Carnie. Like them, she will give voice to the unique perspectives of working-class women—impoverished mothers and widows, unmarried working women, women trapped in unhappy marriages--, but her viewpoint is not "reformist," as the earlier women writers was.[11] It is rebellious and revolutionary, calling for women to define themselves, rather than be defined by their traditional domestic roles.

Carnie draws on these previous works, but her presentation of their shared themes is bolder because she combines the collective revolutionary calls of Chartism with the passionate defense of working women. Living in a time of strong union and women's suffrage activity, she firmly rejects both the sexual division of labour and power and the view of women as the weaker and apolitical sex. Especially in *Voices of Womanhood*, Carnie's poems are a call to action for both men and women as well as a revelation of the lives of working-class women.

The Poetic Achievement

In *Songs of a Factory Girl* (1911), Carnie begins to develop the themes that will come to fruition in *Voices of Womanhood* (1914). One theme is the emphasis on the lives of women, especially working-class women, and, in particular, their roles as mothers. This begins with the book's dedication "To My Mother" and continues in the poems "An Old Woman's Hands," "Motherhood," "The Mother," and "A Tired Mother." The poems are implicitly, though not explicitly, about working-class mothers. "An Old Woman's Hands" is a loving celebration of a woman's toil-worn hands. In addition to caring for children and the ill, something mothers of all classes might do (unless they hired nannies, servants, or nurses to do it for them), the old woman has "with pleasant haste washed the best cups /When some old neighbor called to take her tea /Within a spotless room." In another poem, "The Mother," the speaker says she has "only one dress that is fair" and that she stays in a "bare little room." "The Mother" is Carnie's first use of the dramatic monologue form, a type of poem in which the speaker is not the poet but a fictional creation who reveals both her thoughts and the material circumstances of her life. The dramatic monologue is the poetic form that Carnie will explore intensively in *Voices of Womanhood*.

Another new development is the use of a collective voice to call for action and to envision radical change. For example, in "A Marching Tune," for the first time Carnie uses the Chartist working-class form of a song calling for political solidarity. "A Marching Tune" begins with this rousing stanza:

O, the beat of the drums,
And the sheen of the spears,
And red banners that toss like the sea,
Better far than the peace
That is fraught with deep death
To the wild rebel soul set in me:
Better pour out the blood in a swift crimson flood,
As to music we march to the grave,
Than to feel day by day the slow drops ebb away
 From the chain-bitten heart of a slave.

Here the speaker becomes a part of a collective, a "we" that fights for freedom. But what did Carnie's freedom encompass? At this point in her writing, she does not explicitly describe her goals. But one element was, clearly, women's equality. In 1913, composer Ethel Smyth set "A Marching Tune" to music for the suffrage movement, retitling it "On the Road" and dedicating it to movement leader Christabel Pankhurst. It was sung at suffrage rallies and marches.

But Carnie's vision of a changed world moved beyond the women's suffrage movement. In poems, such as "A Year's Dream" and "Freedom," she writes, "Oh, let us dream/ Of a world where Beauty reigns" and tries to imagine a new world created from today's struggles: "In a hundred years or more they will sing sweeter songs than we know." While this is the goal she works for, she knows it will not be accomplished easily or quickly and recognizes the frustrations and failures that will be encountered ("Looking Back"; "Failure"). In fact, this book of poems is part of that endeavor. Carnie's concluding "Afterword" states,

> You may praise, you may scorn, but my spirit has rest
> In the arms of this thought—"I have given my best."
> I have given my best. Though the poor flowers I bring
> Be not lilies nor roses, but just such as spring
> In the cool, quiet hedgerow, to catch the tired eye
> Of the labourer going homewards 'neath even's grey sky.

In these poems Carnie is no longer writing for the approval of middle-class audiences as she did in her first book. She is beginning to define her poetic voice as a spokeswoman for the working class.

In *Voices of Womanhood* Carnie brings these developments into full flower. The opening "Prelude" promises readers "Voices impetuous, daring, and wild/ Voices of agony, moaning, and fear;/..../ Voices of rebel, or motherhood mild," and the poems that follow deliver on those promises. Some are longer narrative poems that tell of lives destroyed by betrayed love or political persecution ("The Unburied Dead"; "The Heretic"); others describe people whom history overlooks ("The Lost Comrade"; "Unknown"). For the first time, in mature womanhood, Carnie writes poems that argue straightforwardly for women's equality. She sees this goal as something that both men and women need to recognize and work toward. The fourth poem in the volume, "Why?," implicitly asks why women should be relegated to lesser lives and states that women can do everything that men can:

> My limbs are strong to toil from morn to night,
> Or waste in dungeons dark for Freedom's sake,
> And throats as soft and white the rope has strung,
> And hearts as womanly the fool may break.
>
> I'm strong for labour, pain, and heat of day,
> My little hands may fight the vile disease;

And through the darkened vale I bring back life,
And choose the hardship rather than the ease.

Thus, feminism is an important part of Carnie's vision of transformed world, a world that she hopes her poems will help to build.

Carnie's most notable achievement in this volume is using her new-found form of the dramatic monologue to bring to life a wide variety of working-class women. These dramatic "voices" include a servant describing how she lives for "Her Sunday Out" and an unwed mother mourning her dead baby although "the old and wise" assure her "it is best!" "A Washerwoman" defies those who hire and despise her with the words:

What do I care? My pot of beer
Is more than all your praise or blame.
My children died, one after one—
Did I not wash for you the same?
My tears fell fast into the tub
To "rub-a-dub, rub, rub-a-dub"!

Some voices build on the themes present in earlier working-class women's poetry, such as those that examine sexual exploitation. "A Modern Magdalen" describes how her longing to escape a life entrapped in the workroom led her to her present status as "a fallen woman." She explains,

Grey were the walls of the workroom, where, in the summer's heat,
The tired flies crawled so wearily to the drone of the noisy street,
And I heard, to the whizz of the whirling wheel, my own
	heart's weary beat.

And a weary fear did clutch me of growing grey and bent
As the woman who worked next to me with a dreary, sad content,
And who never knew when the sky was blue, and whose
	life was a lengthened Lent.

Here Carnie draws on her own long, hard years of factory work and imagines how they could lead a woman with different gifts to a different outcome:

So I wandered away and left it, and found it easy to go,
With the light of the beauty God gave me, and
	the scorn and the whispers low,
And the door of the friend that was shut in my
	face, and the flattery of my foe.

Other poems, such as "Shame," examine domestic violence. While this and drunkenness were frequent themes in the reformist poems of earlier writers like Janet Hamilton, Carnie deepens our understanding of the roots and consequences of male dominance and abuse. In the monologue, "The Building," for example, Carnie traces the generational damage of domestic violence. In this poem a daughter describes her mother's advice about how to deal with an abusive man:

> "Nay, strike not back—Forbear," my mother said,
> "'Tis woman's part to suffer and forgive;
> To kiss the striker fierce and passionate,
> That gentler, sweeter thoughts in him may live."

The daughter learns the lesson only too well, repressing her anger and learning to lie to men and to submit to them. In this way, both sexes betray the possibility of "justice," and she becomes a "shimmering serpent form, of haunting guile,/ Because I stayed the blow, and learned to smile." In another poem, "Parted," an unhappy wife chooses to leave her husband, not because of actual violence, but because he has broken faith with her. Now, she lives a separate life which her community rejects, but she is true to herself.

Threaded throughout these individual "voices" are poems that forcefully critique the system that creates such poverty, narrowness, and exploitation. The years 1910 to 1914 were turbulent, not only for Ethel Carnie personally, but, more broadly, in the UK and beyond. The women's suffrage movement, under the leadership of the Pankhursts, held mass rallies and engaged in more militant protests, including hunger strikes and bombings. Ireland was on the brink of revolt over Home Rule. The union movement was also in a ferment of activity. The year 1912 alone saw 1,459 strikes. Several poems in *Voices of Womanhood* address the hopes and fears aroused by these storms of change. In "Upheaval," for example, the poem's speaker begins by fearing change and begging the wind: "O, do not touch my house, thou hungry wind,/ For I am calm and happy by my fire." But the wind ignores her pleas and drives her "out into the pathless wilds." The speaker builds a new structure and settles there, but, as she becomes comfortable, this house, too, is destroyed, and, finally, the speaker sees that, to be free, she must tear down all the old structures and live open to change:

> . . . . Blow, blow, O wind,
> And take my house and leave me desolate—
> If I may grow . . . .

But give me over all things, Liberty!
O strong, clean wind, I do not fear thee more,
But rise to greet thee when I hear thy voice;
I welcome all upheaval and all change,
However fraught with sorrow and with pain,
That bring my feet into a wider house.
Oh, hail and hail, thou clean, destructive wind!

Carnie's hopes during this period, and for the rest of her life, were centered on a collective international movement that would peacefully transform society. A number of her poems present her vision of what such a movement might achieve. "The New Commandment" indicts capitalism, expanding the meaning of the commandment, "Thou shalt not steal", to include all kinds of theft—of time, of beauty, of happiness. It announces, "that vital, simple right/ To roses, bread, and life's full undertone" and calls for punishment, not honour, for the "ermined thief." "Whilst One Remains" powerfully claims that each person's individual freedom and happiness are connected to every other's; thus, everyone will remain enslaved by poverty, exploitation, and ignorance until everyone is free of them. "Dawn" uses the collective voice to urge all to work toward the creation of a new world where

. . . the sobbing of children will be turned to laughter sweet,
And Woman will go honoured, noble, wise,
Linking arms with Man, her comrade, as the highway opens wide
When the tears have washed the shadows from our eyes.

Ethel Carnie's poems are important for many reasons. One is the window they provide into the growing confidence and vision of her unique literary perspective as a working-class woman and radical thinker. Among her very first publications was the poem "The Bookworm," discussed earlier in this introduction, in which the speaker is eager to express her enthusiasm for the glories of traditional Western culture. In her 1914 poem, "Civilization," she critiques that tradition's limitations and exclusions and calls for a new inclusive artistic practice, a practice in which "for the first time in this vaunted land/ Labour and Love and Art walk hand in hand." Such literature and art will be an essential part of the transformed world that Carnie worked toward. Her own poems, as well as her other work, are inspiring examples of this new practice.

Finally, Carnie's poetry provides a perspective that has been sorely lacking in literature and culture, that of working-class women. It is a perspective that expands our understanding of past history and present life and sheds new lights on what we think we already know. A favorite poem of mine, "Cinderella: A Modern Version," is an example of this. The Cinderella familiar to us is a poor, put-upon girl who leaves her dirty work behind to put on a beautiful dress and become the chosen bride of a prince. Carnie's new Cinderella, by contrast, is working class, a hard-working servant. When she tries to escape the house, instead of helping her to escape with new clothes and a carriage, this new fairy godmother orders her back to her work and her place. But Carnie's Cinderella refuses to listen, and, although she knows the struggles that await her, strikes out alone on the road to freedom. In a sense, she is a version of Carnie herself, who followed her own difficult path to self-expression and who fought for her vision of a world, not just freed of poverty, but offering beauty and love to everyone.

1 Biographical details are drawn from Roger Smalley, *The Life and Work of Ethel Carnie Holdsworth, with particular reference to the period 1907 to 1931* (PhD thesis, University of Central Lancashire, 2006).
2 Ethel Carnie, "The Factory Slave," *Woman Worker*, 3 March 1909, p. 214.
3 Ethel Carnie, "We Who Work," *Woman Folk*, 16 February 1910 (page numbers missing in the original).
4 Ethel Carnie, "Factory Intelligence," *Woman Worker*, 10 March 1909, p. 219.
5 Ethel Carnie, "Preface," *Rhymes from the Factory (with additions)*, (Southport, UK: R. Denham, 1908), p. vii.
6 Roger Smalley, p. 92.
7 Ethel Carnie, "Preface," *Rhymes from the Factory*, p. vii.
8 Ethel Carnie, "How Colour Is Introduced," *Woman Worker*, 7 April 1909, p. 323.
9 Robert Blatchford, "A Lancashire Fairy. An Interview with Miss Ethel Carnie," *Woman Worker*, 10 July 1908, p. 155.
10 Florence Boos, "Ellen Johnston," in Abigail Bloom (ed.), *Nineteenth Century Women Writers* (Westport, CT: Greenwood Press, 2000), pp. 231-234.
11 Florence Boos, "'Cauld Engle-Cheek': Working Class Women Poets in Victorian Scotland," *Victorian Poetry*, 33 (1995), 51-71.

RHYMES FROM THE FACTORY.
(WITH ADDITIONS),
BY A FACTORY GIRL.

As the weaver plied the shuttle, wove he, too, the mystic rhyme,

And the smith his iron measures hammered to the anvil's chime;

Thanking God, whose boundless wisdom makes the flowers of poesy bloom In the forge's dust and cinders, in the tissues of the loom.

—Longfellow.

I DEDICATE THIS SECOND VOLUME
AND EDITION
OF MY VERSES AS I DID THE FIRST,
TO MY ESTEEMED FRIEND,
W. H. BURNETT,
AS A SMALL TOKEN OF SINCERE GRATITUDE
AND RESPECT.

PRELUDE.

Hazel-nuts ripen but to fall;
The flowerets ope their petals sweet
But to decay, and leaves turn gold
To rustle under careless feet.

There are some poets, in their dreams,
Will sigh for immortality,
And for a name that, like a lamp,
Should light the vast eternity.

If these, my simple lays, have power
To help one pilgrim on his way,
I'll be content, I will not ask
To sing to those beyond my day ;

For other flowers will deck the mead,
And other birds their carols bring,
In place of flowers that bloom to-day,
In place of birds that now may sing.

February, 1907.

Contents

PREFACE.

These verses were put together originally with no intention of publication. From a child I found myself expressing my thoughts in rythmic forms, and deriving great pleasure from so doing, accompanied though it was with a sense of constraint—that I must do so. It was just as a tune that one has once heard and liked seems to haunt the mind and will not be dismissed until entirely mastered. Some pieces I wrote when I was about ten years of age are not included here. I went on "half-time" at eleven as a reacher in the Delph Road Mill, at Great Harwood, after which I became a winder at the St. Lawrence Mill in the same town. I was a winder for some six years. 'Twas in this period that I wrote "The Bookworm," which seems to have attracted the most attention of any of my writings. It was really composed one morning whilst working at my frame. I think it is no exaggeration to say that all my poems came into my head at the mill. It might be as Miss Marianne Famingham said of me in an article in The Christian World, that my occupation had something to do with the rythmic forms into which my thoughts shaped themselves. I am greatly indebted to the Editors of the two Blackburn weekly papers for having printed some of my earlier pieces. They brought me into notice when I had scarcely concluded myself whether my verses were worthy of print. This little volume is sent into the world merely as affording some specimens of what I have written, and because a number of my friends seem to wish to have some of my compositions in a permanent

form. I trust my critics will be kindly and charitable, and will bear in mind the circumstances of my education, which hardly favour the writing of polished verse. Perhaps the prelude best explains my motives in publishing this little book.

Great Harwood, February 16th, 1907.

PREFACE TO THE SECOND EDITION.

Within a month of publication the first edition of my verses, 500 copies, was sold out. Friends importuned me to re-publish, but I thought it better to wait. Enquiries for copies have, however, come from all parts of the country, and even from abroad, and quite recently I have had orders for as many as forty copies in one day. This has determined me to publish a larger edition, 1,000 copies, containing my former poems, with emendations and additions. I hope it may be received with the same favour as the first, and I hope, also, my critics will extend to me the same considerate treatment. I have to thank many friends for kind and thoughtful suggestions, which have greatly improved the structure of many of my verses.

Great Harwood, January 1st, 1908.

THE BOOKWORM.

I own no grand baronial hall,
    No pastures rich in waving corn;
Leave unto me my love for books,
    And wealth and rank I laugh to scorn.

I envy not the richest King
    That ever steeped his lips in wine!
With Count of Monte Christo, I
    Can truly say "The world is mine."

The world of books—how broad, how grand!
    Within its volumes, dark and old,
What priceless gems of living thought
    Their beauties to the mind unfold.

What flowers of genius suffuse
    Their sweetness o'er its yellow page!
Immortal words of truth and fire,
    Echoing down from age to age.

On wintry nights, when howls the wind,
    And earth lies 'neath a shroud of snow,
I draw the blind and light the lamp,
    And in the world of books I go.

I read of glorious Italy—
    Around her name what mem'ries throng;
The land of beauty and of art,
    The home of laughter, love, and song;

Until methinks I hear the oars
    Cleaving the bright Venetian tide,
Inhale the scent of southern flowers,
    And see the gay gondolas glide!

Or through Verona's ancient streets,
    On Fancy's silken wings I go—
Those streets where, in the dim dark past,
    Walked Juliet and Romeo.

I read of Greece, downfallen Greece,
    Rev'rence and awe her scenes command ;
Though she has fallen like a star,
    Her light is shed in every land.

I read of old historic France,
    Where raged the Revolution wild,—
The fountains, streets and boulevards
    Of Paris, her vivacious child·

Then, drawing near to England's isle,
    I read of Scotland's purple glens,
And, ah! the pictures I behold
    Through Fancy's bright enchanted lens.

I see fair Melrose Abbey, 'neath
    The pale sad light of waning moon;
I stand upon the Brig of Ayr,
    I wander by the Banks o' Doon.

I envy not the richest King
    That ever steeped his lips in wine!
With Count of Monte Christo, I
    Can truly say " The world is mine."

For I am heir to an estate
    That Fortune cannot take from me,
The treasure-rooms of Intellect,
    With gates ajar eternally.

The world of books, where thirsty souls
    Drink deep from Learning's crystal rills ;
Where glad perpetual Summer pipes
    Upon the verdant wind-swept hills.

HOPES

How sweet 'tis to roam at the close of the day,
When mothers are calling the children from play,
To stand on some hill with the friend one loves best,
And gaze on the golden-barred gates of the west.
To watch the rich colours steal into the sky
And gleam for a moment, then darken and die:
The deepest of purple, the palest of green,
The delicate pink of the sea-shell are seen ;
But they fade and grow dim in the gates of the west,
As the brightest of hopes must grow dim in the breast;
Yet who that has known them will say when they're gone,
"If they shone but to leave us I wish they'd ne'er shone."

TO THOMAS CARLYLE.

As one who sitteth in a covert green,
    Through whose full boughs the murmur of the street—
The whirr of wheels, the buyer's, seller's voice,
    Is soft upborne—by distance made more sweet;
Some dusty wayfarer who's followed on
    A cool, grey stream that's led to woodland ways,
Sees all at once the majesty of Life,
    It's grace, its beauty flash before his gaze,—
So hung my Soul, enchanted o'er thy page,
    Taking, with thanks, whatever it should give.
Thou glorious Teacher, who did'st teach mankind
    Not so much how to die as how to live.

NIGHT.

Who, who can look from the casement, when the fair rest-
    breathing Night
Has opened in the sky her casket of shimmering jewels;
When the sleepy song of a bird just undulates on the ear,
When lights from a hundred windows but deeper make the
    shadows;
Who, who can behold the Queen of Night, with her radiant
    splendour,
Her peace and her scented sables, her dreams for the gay and
    youthful,
And not feel moved at her greatness, deep, deep to the core of their
    bosom ?

She brings to the weary millions in crowded city tenements
Dreams of the lovely emerald vale, with its silvery singing
    streamlet;
Of the woods with their trembling aspens, and ancient ivied oak;
Of the primrose, nestling cool in the dewy tangled grasses;
Of the grasshopper with his chirp amidst the fern and bracken;
Of the moon, rising pale and clear over the spire of the old church;
And a thousand other lovely things to keep their sad hearts from
    fainting.

She bringeth to the lover tender visions of her he loveth,
Thinking the stars are her eyes, he gazeth on them unwearied ;
Leaning above the rosebush, he draws in his lungs its fragrance,
And fancies it is her breath, and draws it in with deep gladness.
He thinks of the lashes long, sweeping the cheek of his loved one;
Of the lips, with their exquisite curves ; and his chafing soul
    speeds on
And penetrates to her chamber, pressing a warm caress on them.

Night, night, awe-inspiring, when the myriad candles are gleaming
On the pallid faces of corpses, whilst the living around are
    weeping;
When the child sleeps calm and healthy in his clean and cosy cot,
Whilst his mother's breast is ice, pressing the white satin grave
    clothes,
Pressing the shroud, the cold shroud, that shimmers as if
    exulting,
As if it were proud to touch and cover so fair a sleeper,
The cruel shroud that in a few hours will be let down into darkness.

Night, when the coast-lights shine like stars in the fathomless
    waters,
When the snowy seagulls flutter about the out-bound vessel,
When the lantern in the lighthouse casts over the surge a track,
A track of light that the mariners bless when they see it far off,
When the ^fisherman's wife looks anxiously to catch a distant sail,
Straining her eyes through the darkness as she hears the tempest
    howling,
Howling as if some savage beast that did hunger and thirst for its
    prey.

LEGEND OF THE KISS

A beautiful young Grecian shepherdess
One day, when walking out upon the hills
With him, her shepherd-lover, who did tend
Likewise a snowy flock, saw at her feet,
Like marble gleaming white amidst the grass,
All spangled with the tears of early morn,
A lovely gem of vari-coloured ray,
Which flashed its light upon her dazzled eyes.
She stooped at length, and grasped the glistening thing.
Wishing to give it to the one she loved,
Whose hands were occupied—for one did clasp
A hazel crook, the other arm was round
A tired lamb—upon a sudden thought
She placed the gem upon her rosy lips,
And smiling bade him take it with his own.
But in the taking of the gem their lips
Tasted a pleasure which was so divine
That oft they kissed again, and others, too,
Did follow suit, until it came to be
The never-changing fashion of the world.

WAITING.

A lover waited just at pensive eve,
The amorous wind sighed through the orchard trees
Waking strange melodies, the pale church clock
Slowly tolled out the sweet appointed hour;
Then, shyly, one by one, the stars crept forth,
Gleaming like fire-flies on night's dusky cheek.
The sleepy birds were resting on the boughs,
Yet still he waited and she did not come.
A labouring swain went by: upon his back
The rake, yet sweet with heaping up the hay,
And merry children greet his weary steps,
And press his hard brown hand with fingers warm.
The lover saw no beauty in the group
Of children, pressing round like lovely flowers
About a pillar grand—his wistful eyes
Are fixed impatient on the long white lane
That she must come along: in heaven or earth
Nothing so lonely seems as he who waits.
The silver stars have most of them their mates,
In clusters light they up the purple dome;
The grasses at his feet kiss tenderly,
And all the gentle flowers are dew-impearled.
Can she be dead or faithless? As the thought
Bursts on his mind, oh! rather doth he pray
That she be dead than that another claim
The kisses she has vowed should be but his.
For thus is love, the pure, the true, sublime,
Still selfish in its utter majesty.
He sat him down upon a knarled tree trunk—
A fallen monarch of the mighty woods,
And bowed his head despairing on his hands.
When he looked up, lo! his adored one stood
And smiled away his doubting and his fears.
'Tis thus we wait, and hope, and anguished pray,
And when we sit us down in our despair,
Sinking sweet hopes in bitter floods of grief,
Lo! the fair thing we prayed for draws more near.
It may not come just as we hoped 'twould come,
It may steal near by pathways unperceived,
And when the sky is darkest and the way
Strewn thick with briers, 'tis just as well to trust,
To dream a little, and to drop a song—
To hold our hands to those who are more weak,
To cling a little to the stronger ones,
And strike the harp to charm away our cares,
For all things come to him who doth but wait.

FRIENDSHIP.

Here's a bumper to Friendship, come pledge him with me.
   Gay Love with his roses goes sauntering by;
With roses, red roses, his bright curls are crowned,
   And mischief there is in the gleam of his eye.
      Let him go, let him go!
      sweeter we know.
Here's a bumper to Friendship, come pledge him with me.

Here's a bumper to Friendship, no rose-wreath has he,
   And his step is more languid and slow, oh! by far;
No roses, fresh blooming, with thorns deftly hid.
   O, Love is a comet, but Friendship's a star.
      Through the depths of the night
      It gleams ever bright.
Here's a bumper to Friendship, come pledge him with me.

Here's a bumper to Friendship, who looks eye in eye
   So frankly and freely, with nothing to hide;
A safe boat to drift in o'er shallow and deep,
   With no fear of rocks in wild passions fierce tide.
      Clear and bright is its ray,
      And pure as the day,
Or the fair moon that sails in a cloud-laden sky.

GHOSTS.

Yea, there are ghosts—pale shadow-shapes that steal
From out the mournful church-yard of the Past,
Breaking the bond of coffin and of vault,
So strong, nor sod nor stone can hold them fast.
Ghosts of dead love, dead sorrow and regret,
With soft reproachful eyes and faces thin,
Who beat upon the panels of the heart
With pallid hands, and murmur "Let us in."
If thou be one who knows these mournful ghosts,
Lock fast thy heart, unto their pleas be dumb.
Turning thy back upon their burial-ground,
Behold! to-morrow's golden rising sun.

TO THE BUST OF MOZART.

Thou lofty sweet-souled son of Orpheus,
    Whose dreamy strains of richest harmony
Are borne to us adown the tide of years,
    A string of pearls to charm eternally.
Oft, when the shades of evening, soft and grey,
    Flit ghost-like o'er the four walls of my room,
I gaze upon thy image till it seems
    A living, changeful being in the gloom.
The clear-cut lips relax into a smile ;
    The dainty lace-like ruffles of thy vest
Gently upheave, and still more gently fall,
    With every fancied motion of thy breast.
Ah! even thou, whom Genius made her charge,
    Laying her scented laurels, pure and bright,
Upon thy brow, long since fall'n into dust—
    E'en thou hast felt the pain of sorrows blight.
And yet, when all life's sky was dark with clouds,
    Thy lyre was silent not, but music flowed
From its rich strings, like lucid silver streams
    Winding thro' banks where fadeless blossoms glowed.
The end came in the hey-day of thy youth,
    A pauper's grave enclosed thy frail remains.
Thy end ? nay, 'tis not so, 'twill never come
    Until thy lovely idealistic strains
Have lost their power to thrill the world's great heart.
    Then thou wilt die, and only then, Mozart.

TIME.

Man hides the jewels that he prizes most
   In the dim chamber of his beating heart:
Time, grim and ghoulish, knocks with mailéd hand
   Upon its door, and tears its locks apart.
" Think not to flee my power," he thundering cries,
   " For I have laid in ruins mighty Rome;
Unroofed her stately temples to the skies,
   And sunk the greatest ships that ploughed the foam.
Let beauty flaunt awhile her fresh young charms,
   At length beneath my noose her proud head slips,
I sprinkle silver threads 'midst silky curls,
   And steal vermillion hue from laughing lips.
Let Art repair the ravage as she may,
   That hour approaches when the world shall know
The roses that her cunning hands devise
   Have only beauty's mournful wreck below.
Pale student, poring o'er the ponderous tome,
   Solving the mystery of How and When,
A few brief years will blot thy hard-earned fame
   From out the changing minds of mortal men.
Fond lover, wandering in the green-roofed wood,
   What constancy uplooks thy blushing maid!
And how impassioned the lips that find
   Her cheek's soft pink beneath some oak's dim shade.
What is it thou art whispering in her ear ?
   That Love through all eternity endures ?
Fools! with each silver moon that grows and wanes
   I break a thousand of such vows as yours.
Kings, sway the sceptre of your majesty;
   Queens, when your tresses some deft hand-maid trims,
Rejoice in all the glory of your state:
   I bring into the dust Imperial limbs.
Man cries to me * Leave but one tiny gift
   To show my spirit all it once hath been*;
I leave him only memory, bitter, sweet,—
   A telescope to view the backward scene."
So spoke old Time, his looks all hoary, while
   Exulting of his everlasting power.
" What is the use," I heard a sad voice wail,
   "Of Grandeur, Learning, Love, or Beauty's dower?"
And through the twilight Hope made answer sweet,
   "These have their uses, for they upward tend

And elevate the human mind ;
 The chained vault is not their utmost end.
Though Love's star drop into calm Reason's sea,
 And Beauty's sword grow rusty in its sheath,
They do not die : Science, Thought, Poetry,
 Tell us a thousand times there is no death.
Rome's echoes reach our distant country's ear,
 And Learning sheds its beams o'er pathways wild,
Love keeps the earth revolving with new life,
 And Beauty lives again in her fair child."

LINES TO MY MOTHER.

Fain would I wake a song round thy sweet name,
    Which, haply, should endure a year, an age:
I've sat an hour—the midnight chimes I hear—
    Yet white before me gleams the empty page.
Where love is deepest speech doth tongue-tied seem;
    The words like shy wild birds are lingering near,
But fly at my approach, so take the leaf
    With all the song it holds—a heart-felt tear.

DAPHNË.

Her flying feet speed o'er the sacred ground,
Her face all white with horror backward turns
To where Apollo, filled with passion's fire,
Pursues her 'frighted form remorselessly.
Nearer he comes, yea nearer. Oh! ye Gods,
Be now her aid in this most evil hour!
But, see! Her slender form is changing fast
Into a laurel tree : one lovely branch
Is springing from her feet, and now the leaves
Are dancing in the golden light of noon,
And where a beauteous, tremulous maiden stood
Is now a sacred tree. The Gods have heard
Her piteous prayers, and kept her undefiled.
Henceforth the sacred laurel's shining leaf
Shall be symbolic of the pure and great.

TO THE ROWER.

(This Poem first appeared in the pages of *The Clarion*).

So swiftly shoots Life's fragile bark
Into the unknown light or dark,
There is no time to rest and sleep,
There is no time to moan or weep.

Know this, oh, thou who plies the oar,
The scenes thou passest on the shore,
Be they of joy, of peace, or pain,
Will never meet thy glance again.

Soft childhood's banks, where fairies sport,
Youth's last green glades, where Love holds court,
And old age, with rich Wisdom's wine,
For their allotted hour are thine.

Sing if thou knows a song that cheers,
But breathe not in the world's sad ears
The history of thy grief and care,
Which millions bore and yet must bear.

And mourn not if beneath the wave
Thy sweetest hopes have found a grave;
Where 'neath the wave its bright sands shine
Lie hopes more bright, more sweet than thine.

And if by thee some brother float,
With broken oar and leaking boat,
Let him not pass with careless glance,
And deem it all his own mischance.

Help him his shattered wreck to land,
Breathe hopeful words and press his hand;
And press thee on with steady oar
Unto Futurity's dim shore.

WOMAN.

Light woman! the butt of the anchorite's scorn,
Small wonder she's fickle when Venus was born
Of the changeful sea foam, and was rocked in a shell,
To the sound of the billow's melodious swell.

Weak woman ! whose frailty is echoed in song,
Yet who in her weakness can still be so strong
That, where man would die she could suffer and live,
And where man would hate she has power to forgive.

Fair woman! with skin made of roses and milk,
With lily-white hands for embroidering silk;
Made to sing dainty love songs and wake the lute's chord,
With a Joan of Arc grasping the hilt of the sword.

Oh, timid! the sight of a tiny brown mouse
Makes her turn ghastly pale and alarm all the house;
But she stands by to lighten a sufferer's despair,
And beats down the chill gate of death with a prayer.

Illogical woman! she never can claim
To argue without dragging in a friend's name ;
How strange that wise man, formed so rational and cool,
A soft word from her can transform to a fool!

THE GOD OF GOLD.

Oh, a mighty god is the God of Gold,
    His empire never decays;
In every age, in every clime,
    The hearts of men he sways.
He grasps his staff with an ugly leer
    Through the weary backward years,
And the coins that lie in his coffers vast
    Are minted in blood and tears.

Oh, a mighty god is the God of Gold,
    With vassals to do his will;
Greed scrapes the cash with nervous haste
    Into the heaving till.
And this wild song he doth sit and sing:
    " Oh, a mighty monarch am I,
For honour and virtue, and power and fame,
    With ease I can buy, buy, buy!

" In the distant East, where the palm-tree waves
    It's feathery branches high ;
Where hang the luscious purple grapes
    Beneath a southern sky;
In the icy north, where the moonbeams kiss
    The glittering iceberg's side,
I am king, and where the western shore
    Slopes down to the silvery tide."

Though a mighty god is the God of Gold,
    There are things he cannot buy,
That lie beyond his sovereign power,
    No matter how he try.
Canst thou purchase, vile King of Gold, I ask,
    A Bums, a Keats, or a Moore,
Buy a friendship stamped with the hallmark of truth—
    Make a gentleman from a boor ?

Oh, the hearts that Mammon, the Gold King, sways,
  Are made of worthless dross—
Are lighter than the thistledown,
  Which faintest breath may toss.
The rich gold ore of a noble soul
  Outweighs all the rest that shines
In the depths of the river's crystal heart,
  In Klondyke's deepest mines.

When Sinbad found in the secret cave
  Trees bowed with precious gems—
With diamonds, rubies, sapphires, pearls,
  Fit for the diadems
Of Eastern kings and princesses fair,
  He found not so much as he
Who finds in the perilous Cave of Life
  One soul of Fidelity.

He may purchase castles and mansions grand,
  With turret and balustrade :
But the turret and walls at last will fall,
  As things but transient made.
But the heart he buys not, though to dust
  It falls, yet within the tomb
It springs into flowers that deck the mould
  With signs of eternal bloom.

Then let us look 'neath the tinselled show
  To find what is really worth,
For we oft pursue with much earnestness
  But shadows of the earth.
Oh I beneath the polish, the glitter, the show,
  Oft lies but a worthless thing,
While we pass with indifference stones that hide
  Gems fit for the proudest king.

BOHEMIA.

I would wander away to Bohemia,
    That stretches so sunny and gay,
For the people whose feet touch that magical strand
    Never care what the false world may say.
For the wild winds of Freedom sweep over its hills,
And the dewdrops of kindness gleam bright in the rills
        Of the beautiful land of Bohemia.

I would wander away to Bohemia,
    Where Friendship ne'er casts you away:
Where money no longer is at your command,
    And the seams of your coat are worn grey,
But the honour and warmth of the heart have to tell
If you're worthy along with such comrades to dwell
        In the beautiful Land of Bohemia.

THE RICH AND POOR.

My heart is weary and my soul turns cold
With loathing. From all sides a cry for gold
Arises. Men with coffers flowing o'er
Still kneel at Mammon's shrine and pray for more.

More! Though the people faint beneath a load
Of unrequited labour, further goad;
Drive us more quickly up Life's stony hill
Ye rich! that ye may reap more profit still.

Relentlessly, as vinters crush the grape,
Beneath their heel they press us out of shape:
Their brothers, children of one parent Vine,
And care not, whilst they quaff Life's richest wine.

Yes, cradled in the downy lap of Ease,
They quaff the wine and fling to us the lees,
And even dare to talk of Charity—
A whip that cuts the spirit of the free.

Old Mother Nature, she who clothes the plain
With herb and fruit and golden ripe-eared grain,
Provides enough for all Earth's teeming throng:
If some are pale with want *tis clear it's wrong.

It needs no great philosopher to see
Our system's wrong, but what the cure should be
Men wrangle o'er: one fellow talks of love,
And golden streets to walk on up above.

Quoth he: " Ye poor, be patient here below,
Soon shall ye leave this shadowy vale of woe;
Do not revolt, though pale with want and cold,
Soon ye shall walk a street that's paved with gold."

Another cries " Life's but a little span,
Don't bother, be as happy as you can;
Sing, rich or poor, for when this life is past
We all shall crumble into dust at last.

" Yon beggar woman in her tattered shawl
O'er whose wan brow the matted tresses fall;
And yon fair belle of Fashion, courted, gay—
King Death will turn them into common clay.

" O'er one a marble monument may rise,
Telling her virtues to the stranger's eyes;
And over one the noxious weeds may wave—
What matters it ?—they know not in the grave.

" One lives in wealth, in opulence, in style,
In rounds of pleasure do old Time beguile;
The other knows but penury and pain—
What matters it ?—all sequels are the same.

" Hands that have swayed the sceptre, blazed with gems,
Brows that have drooped 'neath princely diadems,
Fall but to dust; the heart most high and proud
Decays beneath the worm-infested shroud.

" Enough ! It makes one shiver, does it not ?
Waste not your time bemoaning your sad lot.
I say to rich and poor, to great and small,
'Brethren laugh now, lest ye ne'er laugh at all!'"

So speaketh one. Another cries with fire,
With all the passion of his soul's desire,
"If Death be equal, why not also life ?
Why should the toil, the suffering and the strife

" Fall but to some ? Each tender bud that opes
Its petals to the sun on grassy slopes
Drinks mom's bright dew and dances to the wind—
Why not thus bloom the flowerets of mankind ?

" Why should our lives from the first breath we draw
Be overshadowed by dark clouds of woe ?
Robbed of the things which make Life sweet and fair,
We droop, as plants obscured from light and air.

"*Our* lives? They are not ours—in this great mart
Our richer brethren play the buyer's part;
Mere chattels are we, at their lightest mood
Tossed to one side as things devoid of good.

" Worn out with toil, through the beguiling gate
Of yonder almshouse pass with feeble gait,
Beneath a roof thy brother's bounty rears,
Drag out the remnant of nigh joyless years.

" But Evolution, fluttering on her way,
Is tearing into shreds these fabrics grey,
Is bound to weave them in a brighter web:
Take courage—let not Hope's bright water's ebb

From out your hearts—it is no idler's dream:
The little tinkling lowly mountain stream
Is swelling to a river, broad and free—
A river rushing on to meet the sea."

A LOVE SONG.

Love giveth wings to weary feet,
And makes Life's bitter waters sweet,
And turns each dreary grey-hued hour
Into a bright exquisite flower—
  The great magician, Love.

When love is ours, within the heart
Hope's sunlit fountains gaily start;
The commonplace events that pass
We view through an enchanted glass,
  And all seems beautiful.

I speak of love that hath its birth
Betwixt two hearts of noble worth,
Which, as the years glide slowly on,
Blendeth two beauteous souls in one
  More perfectly each day.

Love that is love will live for aye,
When noon's gay light has passed away;
Will live and shed its rich perfume
Above the desolated tomb
  Of beauty and of youth.

LIFE'S DUET.

(Written on a thought suggested in a conversation when on a visit
to Shackerley.)

Life is a duet—the Composer who gave
Never meant it to flow on alone to the grave;
Though 'tis perfect in rhythm and glorious in tone.
There is something it lacks when 'tis played all alone.
O, the bow will grow weary before it is done,
And trail out the notes that in swift joy should run;
And often the eyes of the player are wet
Who has stood up alone to play Life's sweet duet.

Life's is a duet—though a string now and then
Break, dear heart, as we play, we will piece them again.
What, though sometimes we clash with a look or a word,
We will tutor our viols until they shall chord,
And our last notes shall die in a sweet stream of sound,
With peace all above us, below, and around,
Whilst his only end in a stream of regret
 has stood up alone to play Life's sweet duet.

Hark! Grandmere speaks up from her carved oaken chair,
And smooths from her brow a thin wisp of pale hair;
It is long since the rose graced her old yellow cheek,
So we hear her in silence and try to look meek,
But your eyes they are dancing, I feel my cheeks glow—
 What was it she said that amuses us so ?—
" Life, my dears, is a trio, and then a quartette,
Till a full-fledged orchestra becomes your duet."

A FAREWELL.

Farewell! Within the heart's dim sepulchre
    We'll lock rose-tinted dreams, untold desires,
And hide the key from all the prying world,
    Till Time has smothered out these youthful fires.

And, on a tablet of pure gold, we'll write
    These sweet sad words, "Alas, they are no more."
A marble Memory weeping at the head,
    And, at the foot—Love, wounded to the core.

We'll gather up Love's rose-leaves, fallen red,
    And of them we will make pot-pourri sweet,
And when from Memory's vase we lift the lid,
    After long years, what scents our souls shall greet.

And we'll remember when they blossomed red
    In youth's lost garden—then so far away;
But whether we shall weep or whether smile,
    Alas! dear love, what mortal tongue can say?

THE OLD WELL.

As twilight's dreamy shadows fell
I wandered by a dark old well;
Stagnant and grey, with mosses lined,
It stood, deserted by mankind.

Once, long ago, that well was young,
And waters clear within it sprung;
But in old age it stands forgot,
And desolation haunts the spot.

The birds sing in the brave old tree
Which stands close by, the melody
Now high and sweet, now soft and low,
Which other birds sang long ago.

The weary traveller used to drink
And rest upon its mossy brink,
And village maidens, sweet and fair,
Sang as they filled their pitchers there·

If you have gifts to some denied,
Make not your heart a throne for pride;
If you are young and fair to see,
Be not possessed of vanity.

Though face and form together seem
More lovely than a Vandyke's dream;
Like flowers which grace a woodland glade,
So surely Youth and Beauty fade.

Though on the highest heights of fame,
The multitude that shouts your name
Will soon forget how great you are
In gazing on some newer star.

This lesson unto you I tell,
I learnt it from the dark old well:
The World's a mistress never true—
Old things must stand aside for new.

THE MISANTHROPIST.

Apart from all his fellow-men
   Stands the dark-browed misanthropist,
And Friendship's genial sun in vain
   Strives to dispel suspicion's mist.

His life is like a barren rock
   That frowns upon a fertile vale—
The morbid thoughts his mind doth breed
   Place him beyond affection's pale.

From off a pedestal of scorn
   He looks upon Humanity,
Delighted that his eagle eye
   Its faults and weaknesses can see.

Quoth he: " All things beneath the sky
   Are fashioned on a selfish plan ;
There is no virtue in the maid,
   Nor truth nor honesty in man."

Oh ! gloomy, cold misanthropist,
   If I could see things with thine eye
For one brief hour, ere it expired
   I'd breathe a prayer that I might die.

But I will sing, " Man is not vile,
   Though in his heart foul deeds are rife,
Above them many a pure, sweet flow'r
   Is struggling bravely into life.

His feet are on the upward path,
   And, though he stumble oft and foil
Each rosy mom that tints the sky
   Must bring him nearer to his goal."

CUFF-LINKS.

(Written on sending a pair of sleeve links to Mr. Barnett, March
    28th, 1907.)

Since Creation's birth, in the breast of Earth,
    Lock'd out from the sun and blue,
This gold has lain, for a reason plain,
    But to make cuff-links for you.
        As your cuffs you link,
        Of me you'll think—
If you don't you ought to do.

There are links that bind my heart and mind
    Invisible but deep,
To the friend who's call awoke my soul
    First to face Ambition's steep.
        Though I win or lose,
        May our friendship's hues
All their early radiance keep.

BABY'S HANDS.

Two little hands, dimpled and neat,
Two little hands, useless and sweet
As the petals that leave the pink rose;
    All the day long
    Idly they play,
What's waiting for them. Who knows ?

Knotted and brown, say, will ye grow,
Soft little hands, like faint-flushed snow,
Scattering the seed all day long,
    Till, 'neath the sky,
    Barley and rye
Wait for the harvester's song.

Dear little hands, how close ye twine!
Will you haul in, dripping with brine,
The rope that has held the ship fast ?
    O'er the sea grey
    And smiling bay
Hoist the signal to the mast ?

Two little hands, dimpled and neat,
Two little hands, useless and sweet
As the petals that leave the pink rose;
    All the day long
    Idly they play,
What's waiting for them ? Who knows ?

THE SPIRIT OF SONG.

One day the fair Spirit of Song
Invisible walked 'midst the throng—
Her fingers closed around a scroll
To hold the name of that sweet souly
And seal it with a golden crest,
Whose song should charm her ears the best.

Down a long street, ugly and grey,
She passed unseen upon her way!
Unseen she passed, but not unfelt,
The proud man's heart did strangely melt;
The miser tossed a coin of gold
Unto the beggar, weak and old.

A Poet, wreathless, heartsick, poor,
Who'd half resolved to sing no more,
As her bright pinions swept the air
Went home and wrote a ballad fair,
Which proved the keystone of his fame
And 'woke applause around his name.

Each stone pressed by the sandal'd feet
Was stamped with holy thoughts and sweet,
And ever afterwards who trod
Upon them dreamt of Heaven and God,
And mortals wondered that their cares
Had slipped away, all unawares.

A beggar woman, pale, sad-eyed,
Sang merry songs of a gay bride,
And in her voice were frozen tears,
And memories sad of happier years.
The Angel paused, then softly said:
" Alas! she sings for daily bread."

A cage was hung above a door,
And, o'er the city's din and roar
Floated the little linnet's song,
But faintly sweet, not gaily strong.
" Music divine," then whispered she,
" Is born not of captivity."

When golden sunbeams softly smile
Athwart the dim cathedral aisle,
The organ pours its holy notes,
And piping treble music floats
From white-robed choristers, that stand
Like visions of another land;

The Angel looked within the hearts
Of those who knelt, and found sharp darts
Of hatred, ready forth to speed
At those who held some other creed.
" Music is sweet," the Angel cried,
" And cometh not where hates abide."

Through a thronged hall her way she pressed.
A woman fair, with gold-lace vest,
Sang soft and low as zephyr's sigh,
But she had fall'n from Virtue's sky.
" Heavenly her song," the Spirit said,
" But, oh! her soul is mute and dead."

She came to where a shepherd lad,
With curly locks and tartan plaid,
Sat on the slope of a green hill,
Where he could spy the glistening rill.
He watched his fold to see none strayed,
And as he watched, sweet tunes he played.

The very birds from out the woods
Drew from their leafy solitudes;
The glistening brooklet seemed to pause,
To hark from whence such music flows;
The fleecy clouds stoop down from Heaven
To hear the air so sweetly riven.

He knew not that a song so fair
Might bring him 'fore an Emperor's chair—
He knew not that a song so sweet
Might chain a nation to his feet,
But careless gave to brook and mead
The glorious breathings of his reed.

His world it was the valley fair,
The simple sheep his only care ;
And when Night dosed the gate of Day
Once more, and home he bent his way,
He knew not, as he leapt the brook,
His name illumed an Angel's book.

A CHRISTMAS WISH.

Oh, that some magic power were mine,
  I'd breathe a fervent wish to-night—
I would not ask for bowls of gold,
  Containing gems of flashing light—

I'd wish for something better far:
  A matchless boon, which, if 'twere given,
Would turn the world, this Christmas Eve,
  Into a veritable Heaven.

I'd wish that those estranged should meet,
  And kiss, as in the bye-gone years—
That joy should sit it every heart,
  And not one eye be dimmed with tears.

Each moment should be stored with bliss,
  And Hope her fairest structures build,
And not one child, this Christmas Eve,
  Should have its stocking left unfilled.

I'd wish that for a few short hours
  Sorrow and pain should quit the earth—
That laughter, love, and song should reign,
  And every soul o'erflow with mirth.

Is not my wish a happy wish ?
  Do you not wish along with me ?
If things were so this Christmas Eve,
  Oh, what a heaven earth would be.

THE PROPHECY.

" Once more unto my darksome tent
   You come to have your future told;
'Tis just six years since first you crossed.
   This wrinkled palm with gleaming gold.

" How I have cursed that evil day
   We pitched our camp upon this sand,
When at the doorway, low and dark,
   A thing of light I saw you stand.

" I saw your gay coquettish glance
   Fall on my handsome Gipsy boy ;
Alas! alas! of all our race
   He was the darling and the joy.

" But sit you where you sat that night,
   And I the future will reveal;
Come, cross my palm again with gold—
   A Gipsy has no right to feel.

" They say to-morrow you will wed
   The young, the rich, and handsome squire;
They say that on these grey sand dunes
   Will blaze all night the bright bon-fire.

" But on your ears shall never break
   The cherry music of the bells—
You'll lie full many a fathom deep,
   Among the pallid sea-bleached shells.

And all in vain shall wait for you
   The fragrant, snowy pillows;
Your bed, 'twill be the wet sea-sand;
   Your coverlet—the billows."

" O, take my purse," the maiden cried;
   " You will not blight my future joy,
Because I lit the lamp of Love
   In him—your low-born Gipsy boy!"

" Ah! hearts are hearts, my lady fair,
   Though high or low is willed by Fate.
And they who break such sacred things
   Themselves are broken, soon or late."

***

42

The bridal eve dawns starry bright,
  The crested billows gently rise ;
The air is full of holy calm,
  Like to the air of Paradise.

Down the broad staircase comes the bride,
  A dream of fairy loveliness ;
The orange wreath upon her hair
  Lies light as lover's first caress.

She hears the laughter of the guests,
  Assembled in the hall below,
And o'er her cheek a blush there steals,
  Like sunset o'er a field of snow.

Then through a window, open wide,
  She steps upon the balcony,
To view once more with maiden eyes
      The heaving of the summer sea·

A gust blows from the sunset clouds—
  Fair Josephine is bending low
To catch the last long sunset track,
  Which fills the sea and sky with glow.

A gust blew from the sunset clouds—
  A fall, a sudden piercing scream,
And lost to life, and love and light,
  Was she, the peerless Josephine.

A shriek rang out across the waves—
  " Some sea-gull's cry," a fair guest cried—
And wildly closed the mocking waves
  Above the bright head of the bride.

They search her high, they search her low ;
  They hold aloft the torch's flame ;
They peer into the corners dim,
  And call her fondly by the name.

O, call her louder, louder still,
  She cannot hear you where she lies;
The surge beats in her nostrils fine,
  Her dainty ears and violet eyes.

They search until the dim grey morn
    Finds them like spectres in a dream;
And ever moan's the wretched groom,
    " O, where is she?—my Josephine."

All, all in vain doth wait for her
    The fragrant, snowy pillows;
Her bed it is the wet sea-sand,
    Her coverlet—the billows.

The sun rose o'er the sea's grey rim,
    And, trembling, kissed the summer wood,
And woke once more upon the bough
    The birds that cheered its solitude.

The sun rose o'er the sea's grey rim,
    And lighted up the wet-ridged shore,
But Josephine's joy-beaming eyes
    Will see it rise, ah! never more.

All sparkling lay the sapphire waves,
    A look of innocence they wore,
As though in morning's misty light
    No lovely corpse they'd washed ashore.

In bridal robes and orange wreath
    She lay, so beautiful in death ;
'Twas hard to think that form so fair
    Imprisoned not Life's precious breath.

Her hair—a shimmering golden veil—
    Trailed all its splendour o'er the sand,
And like a flake of white sea-foam
    Gleamed forth her snowy ringless hand.

The sun rose high in Heaven's blue sea;
    With reverent hands they homewards bore
The bride of Death, and as they passed,
    A Gipsy gazed from her low door.

Yes, all in vain did wait for her
    The fragrant snowy pillows;
Her bed it was the wet sea-sand,
    Her coverlet—the billows.

TO-MORROW.

To-morrow, 'tis a little word,
    And falls so lightly from our lips:
The unborn offspring of to-day,
    Into eternity it dips.

If you've a duty to perform,
    Perform it now, nor hesitate;
Seize light-winged Opportunity—
    To-morrow it may be too late.

If you've a loving word to speak,
    A loving kiss to give away,
Then speak the word, bestow the kiss,
    Not on the morrow, but to-day.

For, when to-morrow's sun shall shine,
    And flood the eastern sky with gold,
The words you speak may fall unheard,
    The lips you press be mute and cold.

HOPE.

Hope is a little singing, dancing fay,
 Bearing a lighted lamp in her fair hand;
From room to room she trips on joyous feet,
 Where waiting for her step Earth's children stand ;
But oftimes, leaping from the shadowy gloom,
 Defeat and Disappointment, goblins dark,
Essay to seize the child of fairy birth,
 And quench with icy breath her lamp's bright spark;
But evermore doth she elude their grasp,
 Though oft the light will flutter and grow dim,
Now leaps it unexpected into flame—
 Some magic power relights it from within.
The Gods immortal lit it long ago,
 To cheer the eyes that wait and watch and weep,
Until we reach the threshold of that room
 Where waiteth Death, to seal our eyes in sleep.

LONG AGO LAND.

There's a land that is called Long Ago Land, my dears,
    'Tis a land that's unknown to the youthful and gay;
To reach it you sail o'er a river of tears,
    While the hair at your temples turns scanty and grey;
And the clouds in the sky of Long Ago
Turn to faces and forms you used to know.

There's a land that is called Long Ago Land, my dears,
    In the dim twilight hour you may see it again—
May gaze on the scenes that the heart has enshrined
    Through a gauzy veil woven of sunshine and rain;
And voices float through it so gently and low
From the shadowy Land of Long ago.

There's a land that is called Long Ago Land, my dears,
    And the scent of its flowers is half bitter, half sweet,
And its birds have a half-plaintive note in their lays,
    And its brooklets flow gently the river to meet;
And more dear to the heart as the light waneth low,
Is the beautiful Land of Long Ago.

WHEN NIGHT LIGHTS UP HER PALACE LAMPS.

The sun sinks down behind the hills,
    Like some great blood-stained shield;
A veil of darkness gently falls
    O'er woodland, moor, and field;
The moon climbs up the dusky sky—
    Lustrous and fair and clear;
And, bye and bye, the silver stars,
    Like palace lamps appear.

The soft wind wakes, in leafy groves
    The whispering shadows dance,
The air is full of melody,
    Of beauty and romance;
And every care and every grief
    Is banished from my breast,
When night lights up her palace lamps
    And sings her songs of rest.

CUPID.

Cupid, so the poet sings,
Is a cherub, growing wings;
From the canvas he has smiled,
Half an angel, half a child;
But some say, and they are right,
He is a mischievous sprite.
You may build a wall so high
That it seems to touch the sky;
Cover it with broken glass—
Cupid all unharmed will pass.
Cold with snows the heart may be,
Like a barren winter's tree;
Cupid, dancing bright and gay,
Lightly sweeps the snow away.
Through the ages, dim and vast,
Like a sunbeam he has passed ;
Through the winter, through the spring,
When the swords did clashing ring;
Burning through the clouds of war
Like a lovely silver star.
But, alas! 'tis sad to say,
Cupid, fair, is prone to stray;
Everywhere he singing roves,
Is not faithful to his loves.
Oft he plants his golden darts
Into frail uncertain hearts,
That, like bees in sunny bowers,
Sip the honey from all flowers.
Hearts within whose radiant sea
Lies that pearl, Fidelity,
Are not lightly won, I trow,
By each arrow from his bow.
If he be a child at all,
'Tis an *enfant terrible.*

THE SCULPTORS.

How like a block of marble is our life,
One we must carve amidst the din and strife,
Which, if we carved aright, would surely be
A god-like form of strength and purity.

The unclean thought, the low and base desire,
The angry word that wakes another's ire;
The vulgar jest, which passing taints the lip,
All are false strokes that mar Life's workmanship.

Think not, oh! youth, the errors of to-day,
To-morrow's grieving tears will wash away;
Remorse is sacred, but it lacks the power
To e'en restore to thee one ill-spent hour.

There is no vice but leaves its tell-tale stain
Upon the heart, the conscience, and the brain;
There is no action of the better kind
But bears its fruit and elevates the mind.

Oh! let thy life be grandly, truly wrought,
By noble actions and exalted thought;
Then it shall tower, beauteous and sublime,
Triumphant over Fate, and Death, and Time.

A TWILIGHT HYMN.

Daylight is dying : her rich garments trail
O'er the sky's pavement like marble so pale;
Venus is climbing the gate of the west;
Peace, with her pinions, o'ershadows my breast.

. All the sad doubts that were born of the day,
Swift, with her bright hues, are melting away;
Passion, nor sorrow, nor joy can I feel,
Only in calmness my spirit doth kneel.

Steal, ye soft shades, o'er the gorgeous sky,
Cooling, refreshing, my toil-jaded eye;
Though all my cares start into birth with the light,
Like birds on the bough they shall slumber to-night.

Harmony, harmony, soft as a dream,
Broods over woodland, o'er meadow and stream;
Only the bells from yon far-distant tower
Break the sweet stillness of eve's natal hour.

'Tis now that the soul dons her mantle of rest,
And it seems as the gateway of mystery were riven ;
And the soul will mount upward on night's purple wing,
As mounts the bright dew to its throne up in Heaven.

WHY MOURN?

Why moan, why fret ? The stream of life—
    Nought can retain it—floweth on,
And every hour we get more near,
    Like swallows darting to the sun.
Though roses shake their petals sweet
In mournful clusters round our feet,
The seeds that drop again to earth
Shall have a new and glorious birth.

Why moan, why fret ? Though Duty calls
    Away from paths where Pleasure pleads;
Though on a narrower, stony track,
    Our wavering steps she sternly leads;
Though stars above look dim and wan,
And bleeding feet must still press on,
Within the heart shall bloom such calm
As brings for every wound a balm.

Why moan, why fret ? Though sweetest song
    Is oftimes drowned in sounds of strife,
Though not so beautiful and fair
    As once we dreamt this vale of life;
He who doth learn his lesson well
Above the jar and shock shall dwell,
As the great eagle, from his home,
Looks down upon a world of foam.

THE MARINER'S REQUEST.

Lay me not beneath the billows,
    All my life they've cradled me;
Lay me not within the bosom
    Of the grand tumultuous sea.
I, who've rode in triumph o'er her,
    Will not have her o'er my head;
Bury me upon the shore, boys,
    Where my Nancy's foot may tread.

Lay me in the pleasant earth, boys—
    Sweeter there to rest and dream
Than upon the wet grey sea-sand,
    Startled by the seagull's scream.
All my life I've been a rover,
    Never, nevermore I'll rove;
Bury me upon the land, boys,
    'Twas the land that gave me love.

Lay me where I'll catch when waking
    Just a faint gleam of the wave ;
Tell my Nancy not to gather
    E'en a shell to deck my grave.
All my life I've been a wand'rer,
    I would wander nevermore ;
I am weary, boys, of roving—
    Bury me upon the shore.

FATE IS CRUEL.

Along the mountain path she came,
    A pretty, gay, Swiss peasant,
And as she drove her goats along
    She trilled a song so pleasant—
Labour her spirit could not fray.
The brown roof of her small chalet
Gleamed on her sight like palace fair,
For Love, sweet Love was waiting there.
 Tra la, tra la, tral la," she sang;
Across the air her music rang,
Reaching her waiting shepherd's ear,
And he rejoiced to know her near,
For love is, ah ! so charming.
For love is, ah! so charming.

Above her towered on every hand
    The mountains peaked with glittering ice;
Upon her right the chalet waits,
    And at her feet the precipice.
She stooped to pick a floweret blue,
All slippery was the path with dew,
And life and beauty slid below,
Into an avalanche of snow.
" Tra la, tra la, tra la," she sang,
Across the air her music rang,
And he that waited in the vale
Hath heard it change into a wail,
For Fate is, ah ! so cruel.
For Fate is, ah! so cruel.

WHEN THE CHILDREN ARE ASLEEP.

(Suggested by the painting in the Blackburn Exhibition.)

When the children are asleep,
　　Sweet the stillness that is born;
When the prattling cherry lips
　　Smile, unquestioning till morn;
When the little hands are still,
　　So mischievous all the day,
And the counting beads and blocks
　　In the play-drawer laid away;
　　　　, the throb of tired delight
　　　　As we hear their last " Good-night,"
　　　　When the purple shadows creep,
　　　　And the children are asleep.

When the fairy-tale is done,
　　And the evening prayers are said,
And the pillow undulates
　　Round each tumbled golden head;
When the eyes that danced and dimmed
　　With white lids are shrouded o'er,
And we turn with cautious steps
　　For a last peep at the door.
　　　　O, the anxious cares that fall
　　　　From the overburdened soul,
　　　　As adown the stairs we creep,
　　　　When the children are asleep.

When the children are asleep
　　In the sleep that never breaks,
And we need no more to fear
　　Lest our voice or footfall wakes;
When there are no tales to tell,
　　No more need to chide or frown,
And the chair no more is heaped
　　With the rent and sullied gown ;
　　　　O, the gloom that lies o'er all,
　　　　Now we miss their good-night call;
　　　　In the dark we sit and weep,
　　　　When the children are asleep.

MY TOAST.

He singeth best who sings for love,
　　Who has no thought of worldly gains ;
The bird that sits within the grove
　　Gives to the air its richest strains:
Cares not who blame nor who give praise,
　　Happy the leafy boughs among ;
It sits and sings its sweet wild lays,
　　Because it has the gift of Song.

A fig for him who sings for gold,
　　Or but to win himself a name;
You'll find his lays are tame and cold,
　　Arranged to please the eye of Fame.
But here's to him who sings for love!
　　Who barters not his legacy;
O'er whatsoever land he rove,
　　I pledge him! Drink! whoe'er he be.

WINNIE LEE.

By the bend of yonder river,
    Breaking sadly on the eye,
Stands an old half-ruined cottage,
    Roof all open to the sky.

Thirty winters, thirty summers,
    Have elapsed since there did dwell
In that cot a gentle maiden,
    Fairer than my pen can tell.

For her voice was like the chiming
    Of the sweet church bells at morn,
Eyes like darkest purple pansies,
    Hair like waving golden corn.

There she passed her happy childhood,
    By the river oft she roved
In her dreamy, peaceful girlhood,
    With the father that she loved.

Never was she discontented
    By the river's rise and fall,
Never wished the humble cottage
    Changed into a stately hall,

Till one summer's day a stranger
    Her rose-covered nest espied,
Saw her gathering slender lilies,
    Blooming by the river side,

Much he marvelled that a flower
    Half so beautiful and sweet
Should be growing, all unnoticed
    In this riverside retreat.

He addressed her, and his language
    Was so courtly and so fair
That she heeded not the river
    Singing "Winnie Lee, beware !"

For he talked of distant countries,
　　Where the sky was always blue,
Where the air was soft and balmy,
　　Where the peach and lemon grew.

Oft they met beside the river,
　　Pearly morn and twilight grey,
Till her young heart, fresh and guileless,
　　He had stolen quite away.

Rumour said that he was noble,
　　That blue blood flowed in his veins,
That he owned a lordly castle,
　　Overlooking vast domains.

Foolish world of narrow dogmas,
　　Fawning unto wealth and race ;
Often those thou christens " Noble "
　　Are the basest of the base.

Noble ? with a tongue of falsehood,
　　Versed in the betrayer's art;
For a fancy, light as swan's down,
　　Thus to break a trusting heart.

For it is the old, old story,
　　Just as sad and hard to tell,
Where the man proved fickle-hearted,
　　the woman loved too well.

As a careless maiden plucketh
　　Some sweet bud which charms her eye,
Toys with it an hour, then flings it
　　In the dust to fade and die:

So he plucked this wayside lily,
　　Robbed her of her pure good name,
Passed upon his way and left her
　　But a legacy of shame.

Oft she wandered by the river
　　With a heart that ached with pain,
Waiting, waiting, ever thinking
　　Surely he will come again.

Autumn glided into Winter,
　　Trees swayed branches black and bare,
Still he came not, and her spirit
　　Yielded unto dark despair·

Then one solemn hour at midnight,
　　When her poor old father slept,
From the shelter of her childhood
　　Like a vision sad she crept,

Till she stood besides the river,
　　Winding on by hill and down,
In its bosom bright reflecting,
　　and pale, the silvery moon.

" River, river, cool and peaceful,
　　Gliding on to meet the sea,
Hide me 'neath thy tranquil waters,"
　　Wildly whispered Winnie Lee.

One short prayer for peace and pardon,
　　Three steps outward from the shore,
Then the current drew her under,
　　And her heart repined no more.

But the bright moon veiled her radiance,
　　And the wind sighed dismally,
As adown the river drifted
　　The dead form of Winnie Lee.

Thirty summers, thirty winters,
　　Have elapsed since there did dwell
In that cot a gentle maiden,
　　Fairer than my pen can tell.

But the waving river grasses
　　Whisper still her mournful tale,
When the yellow leaves of Autumn
　　Flutter earthwards on the gale.

And the river tells it ever
　　To the stars that stud the skies,
When the dews of eve are falling,
　　Like to tears from angel eyes.

TO AN ITALIAN WOMAN.

And is the love for her fair native land
    So slight that 'neath these cold skies she can roam ?
Why, even one who never breathed its airs
    Would joy to call that lovely land her home!

Why was I born with all this love of hue,
    Golden acacia—cerulean skies,
Whilst one who's born in Beauty's very heart,
    Can wander from it with unseeing eyes.

Like some bright-plumed bird amidst the grey
    I spied her orange head-dress 'midst the throng,
And paused awhile to muse upon her fate,
    And wonder why she left that land of song.

The brilliant kerchief folded o'er her breast,
    The heavy ear-rings, proud and graceful mien,
The little bird that hops within the cage
    That plump hand holds, of lively intense green—

All make a picture full of warmth and glow,
    Contrasting strangely with the scene so cold,
As one by one the careless crowd goes by,
    Nor cares to stay and have its fortune told.

Now passes by a lover and his lass,
    Eye flashing into eye, they cannot see
The pensive beauty of this southern face,
    Which seems to me incarnate Italy.

The passion and the langour of dark eyes,
    The rounded contour of the olive cheek,
The bird that picks the dainty fortunes out—
    All to my heart in vivid language speak.

Oh! could I only speak thy liquid tongue,
    What would I give? What questions I would ply!
For as thou look6st at me loitering near,
    Methinks there's something friendly in thine eye.

Ah, nay, sweet sister of a southern land,
    I need no fortune told—I know it well;
But take the coin, 'tis tendered not as alms,
    As from a friend, who in her dreams doth dwell

Full often by the Arno's silver stream,
    Hears the bloused fruiterer praise his mellow wares,
The water-carrier cry 'long sun-baked streets;
    Sees heavy purple grapes and ripening pears,
And gives a slender token unto thee
For conjuring forth a dream of Italy.

HAPPINESS,

Oh, Happiness! what art thou but a myth ?
    A phantom shape our mortal hands ne'er grasp,
A fairy, decked in shimmering flower-hung robes,
    Which turn to ashes as they meet our clasp.
The miser thinks he finds thee in the gold
    He hoardeth up, until the cold dank earth
Enwraps his heart more cold, and others spend
    His cherished gains in revelry and mirth.
Some find thee in the study of their kind.
    And some in vernal woods and purling brooks;
Some think they find thee in a woman's smile,
    Others, again, in wine-cups, music, books.
We see thee beckoning to enchanted lands,
    When we are dreamers in Youth's fragrant bowers,
When all the world is steeped in rosy light,
    And Hope makes gay the path with tropic flowers.
The stoic tells us thou art but a dream,
    And a cold smile doth wreathe his joyless lips;
'Tis plain he ne'er has tasted from thy springs
    Sweet Happiness, or it were but in sips.
But now the moral of this prosy speech—
    This, ode, philosophy, whate'er you will:
He who enjoys himself in pure pursuits,
    In gaining knowledge, who doth nobly fill
The niche where God, or Destiny, or Chance,
    Or all the three, have placed him, high or low ;
Who strives to lift himself and fellow-men,
    Ere out from 'neath the porch of life he go
Into the dusky night the world calls death;
    Who's true in friendship, generous to a foe,
And holdeth honour dearer than his breath,
    Has happiness in his heart, the best,
    The purest and more lasting than the rest—
And when to reign bright Happiness doth cease,
The Throne is taken by her sister, Peace.

THE PAST

(Suggested by Mr. Tattersall Wilkinson's " Memories of Hurstwood," in which are
chronicled the cock-fighting and bull-baiting sports, now happily only old tales.)

Yea, let them go, those dark, old brutal days,
Though History strive to warm them into bloom;
Though wild Romance and Chivalry were twined
With their strange fibres, lay them in the tomb.
A fairer land is stretching on before,
And higher aims, and great and noble dreams,
Save only from the Past the pure and high,
The grand old forests, and the taintless streams.

Where gathered once the excited curious crowd,
To view the torture of a creature wild
Chained by brute brothers, now the village school
Rears its old roof to lead the peasant's child
In higher walks. Better for him to read
The stars that twinkle in their vast array,
Tales of fair lands that stretch beyond the seas,
Than spend the tenor of his life as they.

Yet leave us from the past the castle grey
Which frowneth from the slope of yonder hill,
Where ivy green clings close to crumbling stones,
And each new race of songsters loves to trill.
Keep of the Past the splendid and the true,
And link them with the Present's growing light,
But let the relics of mere brutal power,
Sink into nothingness and deepest night.

Yet even in those days unlearned and dark,
Shone out full many a soul, like some bright star,
Which by its yearnings and its courage high
Hath partly helped to make us what we are.
O, there are ladders whereby we ascend
Unto the bliss of Learning's glorious sky,
Built up of bleeding souls, who for the right
Wove for themselves a glorious destiny.

All honour to the martyrs of the Past,
May their blest names ne'er fade from Memory's scroll,
These would we save from dull Oblivion's wave
Through all the centuries that ceaseless roll.
Who taught that Love should triumph over Force,
That Thought and Truth should tame the hearts of men,
To these, come lift the flowing bumper high,
And drink to them again! again! again !

LOVE: FROM TWO STANDPOINTS.

Blue was the sky as sweet Agatha walked
By the side of the murmuring river ;
The lily-cups floated upon its calm breast,
And she dreamt that Love lived for ever.

Her hair floated down, a sunshiny veil,
O'er her shoulders so slim and so girlish,
And the smile in those eyes of the myrtle's own hue
Might have banished a frown that seemed churlish.

"Oh, where are you bound for, my damsel so fair?"
Said a weary and wrinkled old woman,
With a load on her back and deep care on her brow,
And so old that she scarcely seemed human.

" I'm bound for a spot where one waits," answered she,
" Who has stolen my heart from its casket."
" 'Tis a jewel you'd better get back again, child,"
Said the hag as she shouldered her basket.

" Oh! I'd not have it back for the world," answered she,
" It is happy and safe in his keeping,
And he gave me his own in return for the gift,
And much joy from our bargain we're reaping."

" My child," said the hag, " as you journey through life
You will find that you'd best keep your own heart,
For sometimes you barter a heart of pure gold
And get in return but a stone heart.

" My John was as handsome as he whom you go
To meet in your dress of white muslin,
And he swore he would love and care for me till death,
But things have turned out awful puzzling.

" For I've worked all my life, both at home and the loom,
And tended the children who joined us;
We brought them all up, now they're married and gone,
And not a dry crust do they find us.

" And John now is bald as a parrot in spring,
And can't go to work for rheumatic;
His temper, once sweet, is as sour as a crab,
And I toil like an old automatic.

" I never have time for to look at the sky,
Though we've courted beneath it in t' moonlight;
The moonlight of love now is one candle power,
And we've long since exhausted it's bloom bright.

" So, child, do consider before you proceed
And go on your journey to greet him ;
Don't you think you had better turn back again, dear,
Than be in a hurry to meet him ?"

" You foolish old woman," young Agatha cried,
" Your life has been lead, ours will be gold ;
And Charley has such a fine crop of brown curls,
I know that he never will be bald."

" And how if ever you're short of a meal ?"
" Why, we'd dance round the table together,
Join at the bit, make a sandwich of kisses,
And say it was very nice weather."

" Go thy way," said the woman, " and I will go mine,
For youth is a fool, and age is one,
To think to instil precepts and good sense
In a place made for love, and not wisdom."

THE FERRYMAN

There is a ferryman grim,
   As old as the human race;
His form is bowed with weight of years,
   And furrowed is his face.
Still, he is nimble as in youth
   His duties to perform;
He knows no fear though fierce winds howl,
   However wild the storm.

Chorus—With helm in hand he takes his stand—
        His stand in the vessel's stern,
   And steers his passengers to that land
        From whence they ne'er return.

He bears in his vessel dark
   The joyous, the young, and fair;
He bears the weary ag6d ones,
   Whose hearts are worn by care;
He bears the mighty and the great,
   Reluctant though they be,
And steers them over, side by side
   With direst poverty.

Chorus—With helm in hand, etc.

The beard that sweepeth his breast,
   The locks of his hoary head,
Are white as snow-capped mountain peaks,
   And silent is his tread.
His robes are dark as midnight's shade,
   And icy is his breath ;
His boat is named " The Mystery "—
   The ferryman is Death.

Chorus—Witb helm in hand, etc.

THREE VOICES

Three voices are heard in the wind—
One is heard when the heart is young;
      When Hope leaps high
      To scale the sky
And the myrtle wreaths are flung—
And the voice of the wind is a voice of fire,
Which wakes into passion Youth's golden lyre.

Three voices are heard in the wind—
One is heard in the midst of life;
      To the ear it floats
      With warning notes,
Midst the tumult and the strife—
And the voice of the wind is a bugle blast,
Which tells us the wine-red rose is past.

Three voices are heard in the wind—
One is heard on Life's dull grey rim,
      When pale the cheek,
      And limbs grown weak,
And the eyes are waxing dim—
And the voice of the wind is a gentle call,
Inviting to rest the wearied soul.

LOVE'S WAY

Let us forget—there is no more to say,
Wish we'd ne'er met, and pass upon our way;
    Let every vow be broken,
    We'll keep us not a token
To link our hearts to pale regret.
Love, one last kiss—then we'll forget.

Let us forget—yet, stay! one last embrace,
Wild with regret—Sweet, turn away your face,
    Lest every tear-drop, shining,
    Should set my heart a-pining,
And find me lingering near you yet,
Whispering " One kiss—then we'll forget."

Let us forget—Love's harp in silence lie,
That oft hath quivered to our laugh and sigh.
    Ah! nay, the years before us
    But weave more closely o'er us
Fond Memory's tear-hung silken net—
Though Love be pain, we can't forget.

TO-DAY AND TO-MORROW.

Speak for Liberty, and the throng—
Point your arrows at ancient wrong—
The slaves you plead for will coldly frown
And whisper "He seeks but his own renown.
Why should we war with our destiny ?
Things ever were so, and so ever will be."

Praise the tyrant in honeyed phrase;
Never an interrogation raise
As to whether he's noble or whether he's vile,
The mob will crouch at your feet and smile;
Rivet more firmly each link in your chain,
They will applaud you again and again.

But when the grass grows high on the grave
Of him who spoke for the shrinking slave,
When the cycle of years have oft gone round,
And his bones are dropping to dust in the ground :
The rebel, the traitor of yesterday,
To-morrow is hero for ever and aye.

YOUTH, HOPE, AND LOVE.

Youth, Hope, and Love were fairies three,
    In a cave they dwelt, long, long ago,
In a cave inlaid with the Ocean's wealth,
    And in music the tide's gentle flow
Was borne to their ears as they lay within
On beds of greenest moss and ling.

I ween they lived harmoniously,
    Shut out from the world in their twilight home,
With no sound but the swish of the billows blue,
    And the stars peeping in through the airy dome.
Oh! a tranquil, happy, languorous life
Lived they, untouched by sin or strife—

Till a messenger came from the outer world
    And entered their haunt, and a scented air
Swept in with the folds of his garment soft,
    And they saw that the face of the Youth was fair
For bis cheek had the bloom of the wild dog-rose,
And his curls lay as sunbeams on fields of snows.

And at his side a lute there hung,
    And its strings were made of the finest gold,
And were intertwined with the sweetest flowers
    That bloom in the meadow, field, or wold;
And he took the lute from its ribbon gay,
And sang this soul-inspiring lay :

        " Come away! Come away!
        Too long do you stay
    And list to the cry of the wild sea-mew;
        Too long have you lived
        All alone, all alone,
For the world groweth weary of waiting for you.
Though *tis pleasant to sit in this gorgeous cave,
And hark to the voice of the rollicking wave,
        Ye must leave it and come—
        Hearts are fevered and sad
        That the presence of you
        Would make lightsome and glad.

Then out they went from their lonely home
    Into the world with its wearisome ways;
And Hope ever cheered with her enchanting strains
    The hearts sore petplext within Life's dreary maze ;
And Love scattered pathways with passion-flowers fair,
And Youth sprinkled sunbeams upon the cold air.

BEAUTY.

I dreamt of Beauty when the night was young,
Just as that priestess, gentle Eve, had strung
The rosary beads of dew upon the grass,
O'er which, with wavering feet, long shadows pass.
I know not what it was that woke the theme
Within my mind and wrought it in a dream—
Whether 'twere born as soft charm of the hour,
The incense sweet upborne from sleeping flower,
Or the melodious verses I had read
Just as old Sol sank on his gorgeous bed,
Whose purple pillows, fringed with amber bright,
Fill all the chamber of the sky with light.
Beauty, of thee the minstrel bards have sung
In marble palaces, and kings have hung
Enraptured on thy praises, so I bring
My harp in hope that what has charmed a king
Folk will not be so vulgar as to scorn—
For people follow kings as night the morn.
Beauty belongeth to no age or land—
The world and every hour she doth command.
The Indian squaw, whose dusky velvet skin
Has tattoo marks deftly engraven in,
Whose head is decked with feathers many-hued,
With her glass beads, wandering about half nude
Beneath the tropic sky and palm-tree's shade,
Is just as lovely as the British maid,
Whose silky ringlets hold a sunny gleam
As bright as that with which mom gilds the stream;
Whose eye is like the violet sweet, that drinks
The early dew upon fresh river brinks—
Upon whose cheek there lies a bloom as soft
As on the peach that summer breezes waft.
The Indian Chief would not resign his bride
For one with an unmarked and snowy hide;
And, fancy, how would laugh an English Jack
If unto him you pressed a maiden black!
Oh ! ye vivacious daughters of gay France,
Fickle, coquettish, loving song and dance;
Ye lovely dark-haired daughters of Japan,
Who, flower-bedeck6d, wave the cooling fan;
Ye gems of Ireland, whose bright Celtic eyes
Have caught the glow and gloom of native skies,

And ye bright daughters of the amorous South,
With lustrous eyes and luring carmine mouth,
With smile voluptuous, movements graceful, free—
Exquisite lilies of warm Italy;
And Persian beauties, where the rich red rose
Gives up her breath unto the dainty nose;
Oh ! were the land of Persia desert bare,
'Twere not a desert if you loiter there
To charm the ear with song, the eye with mien,
And sit upon the strip of " herbage green."
Almond-eyed children of the land of Spain,
Stately, yet fiery—loving nigh to pain;
Ye little dumpling darlings that we see
Upon the low banks of the Zuyder Zee;
Ye moonlight German belles, without a flaw,
And stunted fur-bemantled Esquimaux;
All, all are lovely unto someone's gaze,
And someone chants with truth a bar of praise
To every type of beauty that is seen
Beneath the sky upon this earth's bright screen.
Glance o'er the* mouldy pages of the Past,
In Time's dim hall her power has been most vast;
For her great battles have been won and lost,
For her the gleaming swords in duel crossed,
And he who won and stained his soul with guilt
For her dear sake, forgot that blood was spilt
As her white hand lay on his sleeve awhile,
Whilst basking in the bright inconstant smile,
Which on the morrow he might see bestowed
On any of the chosen in the crowd.
Across my mind there floats a bright vignette
Of blue sky, waving palm, and minaret;
A stretch of desert where the pyramid
Uprears its giant form, and, at a bid
From Fancy, starts to life the glittering scene—
I stand before the throne of Egypt's Queen,
Anthony's love, now nothing but a name
Breathed lightly from the languid lips of fame.
Ah! where is all her boasted beauty now ?
The gems that sparkled on that regal brow
Are scattered in all nations, and that eye
Of dew and fire—the dust on it doth lie.
And still as proudly flows life-giving Nile
As when o'er it she glanced with queenly smile.
There is a beauty that doth lie Not in the lustre of the eye,

Nor graceful curving of the throat,
Nor voice of sweet melodic note;
Not in the cheek's fair peach-like glow,
Or tapering hands, white as the snow—
Those fleeting charms which Nature gave,
That Time rolls onward to the grave.
The beauty of a generous heart,
That feeleth for another's smart;
A mind that's gentle and refined—
These are the charms that stay behind
When Youth lies shattered on the stem ;
And when Death comes to gather them,
They leave a memory soft and bright
As the last rays of summer light.

CHARITY

Within a crowded city there stood not long ago
A feeble, palsied beggar—chill, chill, the winds did blow;
But not more cold were they than hearts that passed him to and fro,
Within whose stony channels no streams of pity flow.
His rags scarce hung together, his cheek was blanched and thin;
With trembling touch he fingered his dear old violin,
And strove to bring forth melody with discord all within.

One lady said " Unto these things
It's time folks put a stop ;
One really has no pleasure
In coming out to shop.
My husband's in the Peerage,
When I go home I'll see
If something really can't be done
To check this poverty."
She bought a stylish dinner gown,
Two thousand francs it cost,
And, pondering still the problem,
Unto her carriage crossed.

Then came an old professor,
Honoured and wise and grey;
In the pursuit of learning
He'd passed his life away.
Oh, he could tell the reason
Of spots upon the sun ;
He knew how many thousand years
This earth in space had spun ;
He knew the name of every herb
That on its surface blows;
He knew not how to feel a pang
For these, his brother's woes.

The next, a prosperous merchant,
Approached with pompous mien ;
He eyed the shivering beggar
With just a touch of spleen.
" He need not to have been so poor
If he had thrown Life's dice
With careful hand, or had not been
Addicted unto vice.

Although to see a sight like this
My tender heart doth grieve,
My conscience tells me it were wrong
Such cases to relieve."

Then came along a sempstress,
And shabby was her dress,
And face and form and movement
Showed utter weariness.
She slipped a coin within his hand—
"I'm sorry 'tis not more;
But you are very welcome,
My brother, *Au revoir.*"
A sob rose in his wrinkled throat,
He turned away his head;
The coin, though small, within his hand,
Was breakfast and a bed.

He said, " You are an angel,
Sent down my need to meet."
The angel shook her head and smiled,
Then passed along the street.

LAST DAYS OF POMPEII.

Come, gentle Muse, thy spell and Lyon's ink
Old Time into Oblivion's sea shall sink;
Roll the pale legion of dead years away,
And hoist bright Beauty over dim decay.

*Tis here where marble colonnades are festooned with gay flowers,
Where the cithara's silver voice charms the fleet-footed hours,
The fountain through ambrosial air tosses its silver spray,
The glorious bright-hued butterfly enjoys its little day.
The bright Campanian ocean's cheek is dimpling in the breeze,
Laden with orange-scents the air, and dusky olive trees
Slope down unto the beautiful, the placid, smiling shore,
Where music drifteth slowly by unto the dripping oar.
Serene and blue the melting sky arches the radiant earth,
With every glowing moment some sweet tale of love has birth,
And to the narrow casement, when pale Isis saileth clear
Through gauzy clouds, the soft notes steal to the adored one's ear.
The sleek law-giver, in his robes of purple and of gold,
Stalks proudly through the noonday street, where Commerce doth
   unfold
Her glittering booths, whilst murmurs of a hundred tongues bespeak
The Roman and Egyptian, the Italian and the Greek.
Come, here the pretty harem-girl combs out her silken fleece,
And mark yon slave who, frowning, plans to purchase his release;
And here the gladiator darts with spear upon the boar—
Hark! Through the hot arena throbs the shriek, applause, and roar.
And here some noble poet stands, with music in his soul,
Amidst a fair, admiring throng, his fingers round a scroll.
See, through the ripening muscatels the carven Bacchus shines,
His eye upon the luscious grapes—the God of Mirth and Wines.
Now chime the bells that call the throng unto the rites of prayer,
The candles gleam, the incense burns, the bright-gowned priest is
   there.
Some go to crave of Venus fair a spell to chain some heart
They cannot find the key to ope—to gain a golden dart
That shall like magic find its way through coldest heart of stone,
And thaw the cherished fair one till she vow to be their own.
" Minerva!" cries the student pale, " unfold to me thy truth."
" Great Mars !" the gallant warrior, " keep in my veins the youth."
And thus they pray each one for what their heart desireth most,
Then back again unto the dance, the revel, dice,and toast;
Back to the marbled bathrooms fair, the trellised portico,
The garden where the blooming rose fills the soft air with glow;

Back to their tender, echoing lutes, the bright Falerian wine;
The stately dames with braided air, 'neath which the bright orbs
    shine.
Come, 'tis a feast; the board is piled with fruit and wine and flowers;
Each guest doth wear a chaplet bright as morning's firstborn hours,
For as each guest himself did seat, the ancient custom ran,
A slave should crown his head with flowers before the feast began;
And with the hours of mirth and song their beauty doth expire—
Symbolic of the heavenly things that fade 'neath earthly fire.
In those old days they chose a king who, laughing, did preside
Over the feast, and tell each one when he should stem the tide
Of purple wine, lest he should lose the man within the beast—
A wise, wise law, and one would suit e'en a more modern feast.
And afterwards to everyone the myrtle he did bring,
And call to slaves to bring a harp to him who best could sing.
Harkl on the mellow, perfumed air this careless song doth rise,
Breathing of earth, but in a voice like saint's in Paradise.

    Sing, sing to-day,
    With Care away;
From the unknown to-morrow;
    Seek not a chain,
    'Twill bring but pain
Its darkening cloud to borrow.

    Sing, sing, the rose
    All blushing glows,
That soon, alas ! is faded;
    Nor careth she,
    And why should we
Because our joys are shaded ?

    Sing, sing, the cup
    Doth bid us sup,
And flush our veins with sunshine,
    And Bacchus brings
    Immortal springs
To make our wit more supine.

    Sing, sing, the eyes
    Where warm love lies
Are smiling into ours ;
    Sing whilst the wine is in the cup,
    And whilst our monarch bids us sup,
And bloom is on the flowers.

But, see! across the tranquil sky doth flash a blood-red glow,
On snowy fane, on temple roof, the crowded street below;
Within the breast of that dark Mount[1] the fatal fires awake;
It comes, it bursts o'er land and sea—the terrible Earthquake.
And columns twined with blooming flowers tremble and cleave the
    air,
And eyes where lately smiled sweet Love, burn with a great despair.
The slave no longer feels the yoke that caused the scorching tear,
And private hates are swallowed up in universal fear;
And anguished eyes meet anguished eyes through a thick ashy veil,
And lips all warm with youth and love, horror hath frozen pale.
Each step is fraught with peril deep—they press towards the sea
As to a haven that affords Safety and Liberty.
In such an awful hour as this the miser leaves his gold,
Powerless to buy an hour of life—the treasure all untold.
Earth's bosom taketh back again the rich and costly vase
The centuries again shall give back to the human gaze.
Ever across the changing sky the fire in fury flashes;
The feast, its wine, its king, its flowers, are covered o'er with ashes.
The mother who in placid ease owned not her child of shame
Flies to its cradle in this hour, and feels Love's silken claim.[2]

Oh, gardens fair, and homes of art, and halls where genius shed
Its ambient rays, that time has made a City of the Dead;
Where once the fountain spouted clear, the gnats and lizards play,
And only echo's voice repeats the tale of yesterday.
The morning breaks serene and bright across the purple seas,
But never rings the voice, the laugh, upon the boisterous breeze.
The fame, the glory, beauty, love, dark fate hath clouded o'er,
Only in some poor poet's dream its beauties live once more.
      Vain is earthly pomp and glory,
      This the soul may glean from story;
      From the autumn leaves that sweep
      When the chilling night dews weep ;
      For they flee with Life's sweet breath,
      Swallowed by the dark of Death.

[1] Vesuvius.
[2] See Lyttons' " Last Days of Pompeii."

THE SEARCH.

I sought for freedom in the glorious woods,
    It's leafy banners veiled the summer sky;
I sank me down upon the streamlets marge,
    And thought that surely here her home must lie.
But as I mused there came the bark of curs,
    And through the covert broke a startled deer ;
Her quivering, graceful form fell 'neath the gun,
    And then I knew that freedom dwelt not here.

Then entered I a palace fair and grand.
    A weeping woman met my earliest view,
And, as I wondered what her grief might be,
    She held unto my gaze a tiny shoe.
" Men envy me," she cried in anguished tones;
    " I'd barter all, my land, my power and wealth,
To be yon peasant girl who trudges on,
    And hugs unto her breast one child of health."

Within another chamber sate a man :
    I marvelled at the care upon his brow ;
His coffers overflow around his feet,
    And at his look a hundred minions bow.
" Why do you look so sad ?" I questioned him,
    " You, who have but to stretch your hand and choose,"
And, like a knell, these words came to my ear,
    " Alas! I fear for all I have to lose."

Then entered I within a low-roofed cot.
    A woman grumbled through her househould ways.
" You've nought to lose," I said, " what aileth you?"
    Said she, " One problem fills my nights and days ;
For, ah ! there are so many mouths to feed,
    And in the cupboard is so little bread."
Then sadly turned I from the cottage door,
    And thought that surely Freedom must be dead.

But as I sauntered down a leafy lane,
    A whistling schoolboy passed me, all elate
He ran to join the lads upon the green,
    And gaily leapt he o'er the rustic gate.
A tattered cap adorned his curly head,
    And in his eye reposed the Heaven's own blue,
And as he passed me by the old pink thorn,
    I knew 'twas Freedom's self that met my view.

TO A CHILD.

Little winsome-featured child,
Weeping o'er a broken toy,
If thou liv'st thy heart must mourn
Many a broken dream of joy.

Now thy tears, like April showers,
Quickly come and quickly go ;
But within our grown-up world
With what bitterness they flow.

Thine gush forth so easily,
From the brooklet fresh and fair;
Ours are drawn from sunless depths
 Of that river named Despair.

Little eager bright-eyed child,
Revelling in fairy lore,
Where the prince and princesses
Happy lived for evermore ;

As thou leav'st sweet childhood's isle,
Where the silver wavelets swell,
Time will teach thee that the heart
Cannot always happy dwell.

HETTY SORRELL

(Suggested by the Picture in the Blackburn Museum.)

Through the wild wood she comes with flying feet,
    The frenzy of despair in her sweet eyes,
Her hands pressed to her ears to keep away
    The haunting plaintiveness of its sad cries.
Away! away! from that dark stagnant pool,
    Upon whose marge the sedge and mosses grow,
Where one lone willow bends to see itself
    Dimly reflected in the depths below.
And through the branches o'er her head
    The weary wind goes sighing—
" Away! away!" All through the wood
    She still can hear it crying.

The wild rose bloom has left her cheeks; her lips
    Drop at the corners like a frightened child's;
She runneth blindly as the startled deer
    Runs when a stranger's foot breaks on its wilds.
The swallow's twittering pierces her dull ear
    Like distant music which was once held sweet,
And the warm sunlight filters through the eaves
    Where interlacing branches gently greet.
The fern and bracken 'neath her feet
    Give forth a gentle sighing—
" Away! away!" All through the wood
    She still can hear it crying.

Oh, happy days, ere vanity had power
    To lay beneath her feet the evil net,
How far away ye seem in this dark hour.
    When Toil and Peace and purest joys were met
To make a fragrant garland for the heart;
    Where Innocence, a snow-white dove reclined,
Care was but as a shade, thin as the air,
    Which seldom visited her girlish mind.
A thousand demons seem to taunt;
    The echoes keep replying.
"Away! away!" All through the wood
    She still can hear it crying.

Hush, haunting voice. Wilt thou for ever ring ?
  Wilt thou still wail through all the flight of time ?
Ah! yes ! through all the weary countless years,
  That like a barren heath stretch on, for Crime
Brings retribution in that plaintive note
  Which thrills the air with horror and complaint.
'Twill never die upon her ears until
  Reason and Life have sunk into a faint·
A bullfinch on the tasselled bough
  Mocks her as she goes flying,
Seeking a spot where Peace doth dwell—
  But still she hears it crying.

MEDITATIONS IN HOLYROOD PALACE: QUEEN MARY'S BED CHAMBER.

Sentinel-guarded here hath slept a Queen !
This vilesome pillow, where the grey moth feeds,
Then finest cambric, warmed her fair, proud head.
And she would dream, I wis, of those she loved,
And, waking in the midst of Night's dark heart,
Would hear the sentry pacing by her door.
Sleep, sleep, and dream! just as her weary maid,
Who'd crawled to bed with eyes a-sore for sleep ;
But she, upon a bed of humbler mould,
Would rest secure from all the dangers dire
That waited for that fair, unhappy head.
No throbbings of the heart would wake her rest
When through the chamber pealed the midnight hour.
The tapestries that grace these ancient walls,
Fast crumbling 'neath the chariot wheels of time,
Were then resplendent with a thousand forms
Of horse and warrior, worked in golden thread ;
But now the threads are broken, and one scarce
Can tell the horseman from the fallen steed.
Here is her work-box: once her dainty hand,
Like a white lily, sorted out the silks,
And strove to while away the tedious hours
By 'broidering roses, stiff and far apart,
Upon the margin of rich cloth of gold.
But now the hand, the roses, and heart
That brooded o'er them, winning a respite
From cankering Care awhile, are only dust.
And if you went within the vault of her
Who braided with proud care her silken hair,
You could not tell the difference 'twixt the two,
For Death, like Love, doth break all barriers down—
Death, that great river, waiting to bear out
The gilded galleon and the fisher's boat.
Here is her mirror: once it imaged forth
A countenance so haughty, sad and pale,
Set in a frame of golden hair ; a neck
That rose so swanlike from the ruffle white.
But now the mirror hangs upon the wall,
Its silver worn away, it would not serve
To mirror your small finger. Mark the bed,
Its crimson covering, which, a placard says,

You must not touch, for 'tis " Queen Mary's bed."
Queen Mary's bed ! Ah ! nay, 'tis hers no more:
It is the bed of Ruin and Decay.
The sentry trampeth still, and casts his eye
Upon the tourists who approach too near.
Ever they come, the curious crowd, to view
The crumbling fabrics, hallowed by—a name.
Alas ! what boots it to be called a Queen ?
To wear a little while the silken robe,
To clasp the sceptre in a jewelled hand—
And have the scaffold waiting for your head !
So do these thoughts throng through my busy mind,
As Echo in her hollow voice repeats
The footsteps ringing on the narrow stairs,
The oaken floor, up to the panelled roof.
And what is Fame ? a bauble that is bought
With fear and toil and danger—sometimes life;
An echo that a little while doth wake
The ripples on the placid pool of years,
Then dies and leaves no image on the glass.

TO MY DEAR FRIEND MISS M. A. PILKINGTON.

Dost remember the day that we first met, my dear ?
　　That fair milestone on Life's stony track,
Where we clasped hand in hand with a friendship so true,
　　It has never once thought to turn back.

We have built many a castle with turrets so grand,
　　We have dreamt many a dream bright and fair;
We have drank with glad lips from the fountain of joy,
　　And have shared every burden of care.

When our castles lie shattered—when Father time proves
　　That the dreams we indulged in were vain,
Still our Friendship, my sweet, like some beautiful gem,
　　Shall its joy-giving lustre retain.

When the autumn winds sweep through the fast-waning woods,
　　And do tear from its stem Youth's rich rose,
Then our Friendship shall bloom as the blue gentian flower
　　Shines out from the cold Alpine snows.

RESURRECTION

Once more adown the winding paths of Time
　　Comes maiden Spring with lightsome fairy feet;
Wherever she imprints her dainty step
　　The dark old earth bursts into blossoms sweet.
The torrent, swollen by the heavy rains,
　　Pours through the emerald vale its foaming flood,
Whilst primrose, violet, and pale cowslip
　　Bestrew the mossy carpet of the wood.

Nature designs that all things should be glad.
　　The birds that twitter in the budding trees
Are blythe, and every little flower seems fain
　　To live and give its fragrance to the breeze.
But in the city's courts and alleys dim,
　　Where Want and Vice, those ghastly phantoms, glide,
Hundreds of children languish day by day,
　　Feeling no pleasure in the gay springtide.

Wan children of the city, ye whose lives
　　Flow on like sunless rivers to the sea,
When will the springtime of your hopes draw nigh ;
　　Will it be soon; oh! will it ever be ?
Poor little lives, all desolate of joy,
　　Cramped, narrow minds, homes of dark ignorance,
When will the springtime of a brighter day
　　Dawn unto you, and break your spirit's trance ?

I love you, stunted children of the slums,
　　Though you are neither pure, nor sweet, nor fair!
How can you be ? The purest flower that blows
　　Would be polluted by so vile an air.
I love you, and I dare to prophesy
　　A glorious epoch that shall dawn, and bring
Into your lives the sunny atmosphere,
　　The fresh green loveliness of virgin Spring.

FAME.

"I consider happiness and fame as incompatible."
Miss Helen Matthers, in *T.P.'s Weekly*.

Fame is a bauble dearly bought
    With patient toil and anxious fears—
A voice of praise Time changes oft
    To silence or to jeers.

A dew-drop on the bough of Life;
    One moment sparkling in the sun,
Whilst birds are carolling around:
    Another—and 'tis gone.

A lovely wanton, whom men woo
    With tears, with pleadings and caress;
But as she yieldeth more and more,
    They prize her less and less.

Until, the longed-for height attained,
    They look them down with lips grown pale,
With misty eyes, and sadly sigh
    " Ah! happy was the vale."

THINK NOT WHEN MEN SMILE.

(Will go to the tune of " Believe Me if All those Endearing Young Charms.")

Think not when men smile they are strangers to pain,
    For some souls forth in brightness will walk,
And hide every wound 'neath a garment of mirth,
    As the Spartan boy under his cloak.
Can you tell if the laugh wings its way from the heart ?
    Oh, the brightness that gleams in the eye
May be glaciers of grief, that shall melt into tears
    When the keen, watchful crowd has gone by.

Brightly sparkles the sea 'neath the summer sky's blue,
    And the merry waves dance on the shore,
But the wrecks that are hid in its great beating heart
    And the corpses its sheen covers o'er.
Every heart is a sea, and we never can guess
    What is hidden beneath its bright wave,
For the gay-tinted shell that the tide leaves behind
    Nothing tells of the mariner's grave.

You may walk in the garden at morn's pearly hour,
    And gaze on a beautiful rose,
Which seems to outvie in its splendour the rest,
    Whilst its leaves round a canker-worm close.
And this earth has some souls just as bright and as brave,
    Who can smile where another would groan,
And who show to the world all the sun of their lives,
    Whilst they weep in the shadows—alone.

CASTLE BUILDERS.

Children on the sea beach sand,
Often have I seen you stand,
With shining eyes and spade in hand,
      Castle building·
Though the walls be broad and steep,
Hither comes the mighty deep,
Your creations fair to sweep,
      Little castle builders.

When the tide goes back once more,
Laughing you will crowd the shore,
Yet more eager than before,
      Castle building.
Higher yet, with childish hand,
You will heap the golden sand,
Thinking that it may withstand
      Worlds of water.

Who has not his cherished dream,
Who no memory-haunted scene,
Who no golden " might have been,"
      Hidden deeply ?
We forget our previous pains;
Hope, the architect, remains;
Ever, on Life's wave-swept plains,
      We are castle building.

WHO ARE THE GREAT.

Who are the truly great ?
Are they the gifted ones
Who leave recorded on the scroll of fame
The letters of an almost worshipped name ?
The sculptor, who cuts from the solid square
Of marble white a figure that is fair;
The painter, who makes the rough canvas gleam
With heather-mantled hill and crystal stream;
And the composer, who compiles such notes
As on the ear like seraph music floats—
    Are these the truly great ?

Who are the truly great ?
Are they the warriors brave
Who lay siege to great cities and fair towns,
Who stain with human blood the grassy downs,
Who crush down pity as they boldly fight
To add a city to an Empire's might;
Who, when the wreath of smoke has rolled away,
Look upon heaps of bleeding brother-clay,
Then plunge with fury once more at the foe,
To victory or death, with a wild glow—
    Are these the truly great ?

Who are the truly great ?
I saw upon the street
To-day two urchins in the gutter fight;
And one was thin and pale with want and fright;
The other—a great hulking rascal—fought
A smaller lad, when, quick as thought,
Another boy stepped in and laid him low,
Saying, " Yer oughter fight yer size, yer know."
The rags upon him clothed a hero grand!
He had no cultured language at command—
    But he was truly great.

They are the truly great
Who oppose might with right;
Though two miles from the threshold of their home
Their name is never heard; though all unknown
Save to their kindred and a few dear friends,
Their life proceeds unto its journey ends ;
Though back into the sea of time they pass,
Leaving no flower or ruffle on its glass,
Like the poor herb that sways upon the wind,
Unnoticed by the masses of mankind,
    They are the truly great.

THE ROSE, THE CLOUD, AND THE SUNBEAM.—A FABLE.

Said the rose to the sunbeam,
" Nay, vex me no longer,
For how can I give what I've given before ?
Pass on to my sisters,
More fair and more blooming;
Yea, go, tender sunbeam, and vex me no more.
Though bright is thy presence,
And gentle thy pleading,
They wake in my bosom but pity and scorn.
Thou comest too late,
For I gave my one dewdrop
To a grey cloud that stooped down and did woo me at morn.
More gloomy the cloud,
Yet he sails high above thee;
And what I have given I can never recall.
So the clouds have my dewdrop
For ever and ever,
Till on the great mountains, dissolving, they fall."

SUMMER-TIME.

Sweet is the Summer-time
    When flowers around us bloom ;
When sings the nightingale,
    Throned high in leafy gloom.
When skies are bright and blue,
And all fair things seem true ;
When Hope's gay garlands twine—
When Love is in its prime.

Sweet is the Summer-time,
    But, ah ! how quickly past;
Soon green and tender leaves
    Fly withered on the blast.
Winds howl, and falls the snow;
Sadly the brooklets flow ;
Making a mournful rhyme
With the bright Summer-time.

Fair vanished Summer-time,
    When hearts are gay and young ;
Memory a magic veil
    Round thy dear form has flung.
When leaves lie grey and sere
On their white wintry bier,
Memories of thy fair prime,
Haunt us—loved Summer-time.

LOVE AND TIME

Under Life's hedge paused the old pedlar, Time,
His garments were stained with the dews of each clime;
He had been in the north, he had been in the south,
  the heavy rains drip, where the corn dies of drouth.
He had loitered in country, and danced through the town;
With the sun and the breezes his cheek was quite brown.
At his side lay a pack full of toys fair and strange—
Births, deaths, and love-fancies together did range.

Then he took up his staff, and he shouldered his pack.
" I have come a long way, but I must not look back.
Oh, I wonder, Old Time, if you ever were young,
If ever in childhood your cradle was swung;
I cannot remember. I wonder still more,
Old Time, if your rovings will ever be o'er;
It has been a long day and a wearisome quest,
Will the hour ever come when I lie down to rest ?"

Two lovers then spied him, whom Fate tore apart,
Though lip clung to lip and heart pulsed unto heart,
And the youth thundered "Stop!" and the maiden wept " Wait";
But the pedlar just laughed " I've to open the gate
For the flight of a soul. I've a cradle to fill,
And I can't stop the world for two folks on the hill.
And, though they implored, down the hillside he sped,
His weary eyes fixed on the white road ahead.

POSTLUDE.

I have given my best! I have gathered each thought
From my heart's changing garden, and to you have brought;
You may praise, you may scorn, but my spirit has rest
In the arms of this thought—I have given my best.

I have given my best! Though the poor flowers I bring
Be nor lilies nor roses, but just such as spring
'Neath the cool, quiet hedge-row, to catch the tired eye
Of the labourer going homeward 'neath even's grey sky.
He may crush 'neath his heel, he may warm in his breast,
It is all one to me—I have given my best.

SONGS OF A FACTORY GIRL

To My Mother

CONTENTS.

FOREWORD.

YOU who have clasped Life close, and known
    How great it be, despite of wrong;
The cark of care, the pang of pain,
    I greet you with this Book of Song.

You who have held Love fast, and known
    How fair, although to fall ere long,
As drift rain-beaten blossoms down,
    I kiss you with this Book of Song.

You who have fighting failed, yet known
    Victory was certain, soon or long;
The heart unquelled, the conqueror's heart,
    I hail you with this book of Song.

You who have gripped Death hard, and known
    Till choked with mist, the sun shone strong
On woods and lives unfolding fair—
    I speak you with this passing Song.

Ethel Carnie.
Great Harwood,
· February 19th, 1911.

LIFE AND SONG.

My soul hears melody in many things—
    For this I thank the gods each hour I live.
Should Sorrow shade each joy with brooding wings
    All through my life, whilst Fate to me shall give
An ear to list the song that Nature old
    Has chanted through the ages, I shall say,
Though friends desert, and Time turns all the gold
    Of love to grey, that it is sweet to stay.

Yea, clinging to the skirts of Mistress Life,
    Methinks, a child, I'd hide my face from Death,
Crying, " Whilst woods with birds and flowers are rife,
    And all the air is rapturous with the breath
Of summer younglings, let me stay; but come
    When trees are leafless, and the air is chill,
And the thick ice has muted and turned dumb
    The stream that played beneath the windy hill.'

Yet, even in the winter, song lives on,
    The crackling faggots play a merry tune,
The sparks count time, and cheerily anon
    The cricket doth accompany. Rich June
Has left her ghosts of trembling ferns and flowers
    Upon the pane, and glistening in the light
Of rosy fire that dares the cold's worst power,
    They bring us many a dream of past delight.

And the vast ocean, lashed to creamy foam,
    Tossing to heaven rebellious founts of spray,
Rages and boils, whilst the wild seagulls' scream
    Rings wierdly up into the dome of grey:
This, too, is music—of a grander note—
    Not the sweet bubble of a lullaby
From rosy wave-nymphs, but the brazen throat
    Of Tempest roaring out that men must die.

O Life, for me so full of leaf and bud—
    A harp wreathed round with roses, with the dew
Of purest hopes besprent—Life, with thy woods
    Sweet with the bursting of the violets blue,
I pray thee, should my spirit's ears grow dull
    In age, O! let me singing, laughing go
In leafy summer, when the air is full
    Of mellow breathings, and the roses blow.

AN OLD WOMAN'S HANDS.

Hands, I would kiss you passionate and fond.
　　Lay on the withered brown my youthful lips
In adoration! or would paint them so,
　　Shaking and old, with the worn ring that slips
Forward on the thin finger; men have limned
　　Subjects less noble with a world of care.
What tasks you have performed with patient skill
　　Since the dear days when you were young and fair
And fluttering in a lover's tender clasp
　　Like wild birds caught! You have lain cool as eve
On aching, fevered brows; and cradles swung
　　To melodies that grown men cherish still,
Somewhere in the wild world, no longer young;
　　And with what pleasant haste washed the best cups
When some old neighbour called to take her tea
　　Within a spotless room, and you have dodged
Old bonnets up like new ones—merrily!
　　To me you are more sweet than softer ones
Trembling o'er letters full of Love and Spring
　　And life untried—dear, shaking, year-creased hands
Where shines the almost breaking wedding-ring!
　　A few more tasks are left you to perform,
A wee, wee trembling more—then long, sweet rest,
　　And couched on lace and satin you will lie,
Your history folded on the quiet breast.
　　But we shall sigh to think you did not hold
The flowers of life before we crossed them so;
　　You should have had more roses years agone,
'Tis late to give them when you will not know.

LOVE AND POVERTY.

Go by me, Love, with roses crowned,
  And ardent eyes with pleading wet;
Thou art not made for such as I—
  Pass on! I cannot dare it yet;
Should baby lips cry out for bread,
  And silent wifely look of woe
Burn to my soul, I'd hate thee, Love,
  Who wooest me lo't—so, turn and go.

If I must suffer, let me walk
  Through Life alone, nor pass the cup
To other mouths as yet unkissed—
  And sometimes in the dark, look up
With ecstacy about my heart,
  That, by the path of thorn and stone
I drew no other tender feet—
  But walked without thee—and alone!

Nay, plead no more; thy subtle words
  Of fire and dew are battering down
The walls I raised around my heart,
  As warriors sack a weak, worn town.
Draw near, dear Love, to Palace gates
  Where almond blossoms rosy rain
On marble pavements, and the spray
  Of silver fountains falls again.

Or, if thou finds no entrance there,
  Go further still until thou find
Some dwellers neither rich nor poor,
  And cheerfully reposed in mind;
And some day, Love, come back again,
  With blossomed chaplet, lashes wet,
When Poverty is not a crime—
  And I am thine—do not forget.

WONDERMENT.

To me 'twill ever be a wondrous thing
    That lilies creamy come, and roses red;
That there are mossy carpets for our feet,
    And starlit skies o'erhead,
And princely rivers that eternal flow;
Wild mountain ravines where the cold white snow
By years unmelted thrones the gentian blue,
Which in its heart receives pellucid dew.

Each tiny leaf that opens to the morn,
    Each waxen star of elderberry white,
And every wandering wind doth send my heart
    Into a sweet delight:
Nor all the books of old philosophy
Can ever still that wonderment in me;
Nor all the works of science ever writ
Explain to me the heavens with vast suns lit.

Oh, let me ever wonder whilst I live,
    Like a fair child whose mind for ever grows:
Who ever questions plies, and views with awe
    The rain-drop in a rose;
For those who have that charm can ne'er grow old,
And dreams about their souls shall ever fold.
Who steps aside lest back into the sod
He crush a violet, closely lives with God.

CLOUD MOUNTAINS.

Could we but climb those cloud-slopes, you and I,
Of pearl and opal tints flung 'gainst the sky
When dove-eyed evening whispers in the grove—
We'd never wander back, but live and love
Far from this world with spirit grown so cold,
Methinks 'twould even sell the bars of gold
Warm sunset gives us, and the stars below
So brightly glimmering. Lightly would we go,
Until we rested in a pleasant hollow
'Twixt virgin hills; from ledge to ledge I'd follow
Your daring footsteps, till upon our ears
There smote no echo from this world of tears.
Then would we sit together whilst the stars
Wheeled swift around us like to crystal cars;
And when Night flung her veil o'er each white peak,
Sleep soft together, leaning cheek on cheek,
The peddling earth a speck beneath our feet—
And live a fuller life, more fair and sweet.

IF I FORGET.

If I forget the souls in the Abyss,
    Whom our gold-greedy world has sold to Lust,
May my own soul ne'er leap to Love's pure kiss,
    But trail its broken pinions through the dust,
If I forget!

0 souls shut out in utter starless gloom,
    Hated, and scorned, and starved—if I forget,
Let there fall down on me eternal doom,
    My eyes for ever weep, and still be wet,
If I forget!

MOTHERHOOD.

Here break the strong, tumultuous waves of pain,
 Thundering with awful sound along the strand,
Through which the distant sky looks ashen pale,
 And floats no whisper from the lovely land
Where corn is springing green beneath the sun,
 Where the sweet spray is bent by some glad bird,
Where white moons peep through aisles of plumèd woods,
 And rain-drops, pattering hail, earth's songs are heard.
Down, down, as goes the diver through the flood,
 Where unknown horrors through the waters creep,
Alone, for none may follow if they would,
 Leaving the world with one adventurous leap—
Then up and up, flung back upon the shore,
 Clasping the precious cup of life's pure gold—
Forgetting, as the sunlight makes it blaze,
 The weird, black tides, that o'er the diver rolled.

THE MOTHER.

I am tired, yet I pass not to rest;
    I am weak, yet my love makes me strong;
And you never would weariness guess,
    As I croon my last darling a song.

Such a queer little song of the moon,
    And her pranks in the realms of the skies,
That I learnt in my own mother's lap—
    And he looks with his big, wondering eyes.

When I open the door to the sun
    I can catch the low hum of the street,
Where the gay girls unmarried, go by,
    With their laughter so careless and sweet.

I have only one dress that is fair,
    And I stay in my bare little room,
But the glint of my last darling's hair
    Lights the place like the golden of broom.

All my ribbons have gone for his sleeves,
    That I wore in light days long ago!
But the little blue beads on his neck
    Are like gentian flowers up in the snow!

I would climb the steep path up the hill,
    I would lie where the heather is blue,
But the warm, wee hands pull at my skirts—
    And so what is a woman to do?

I will wait till his feet have grown strong,
    For the bleak, ragged, beautiful moor—
I will sit in my little grey room
    Till my darling can run through the door.

Then together we'll climb the hill-path
    With the stones rolling down the sheer steep
And I'll watch the light leap in his eyes
    As a ship o'er the rim of the deep.

I will say, " Little boy, this is Life!
    From the sod to the far, boundless blue!
'Tis a sweet and a brave, (little boy),
    And a great world I've given you to."

A TIRED MOTHER.

Hush, prattling younglings, wake her not awhile!
    The hueless day has left its trace behind—
Her lips are softened in a tired smile;
    In some sweet spot doth roam her happy mind,
For a few moments from its cares set free
And breathing the soft airs of liberty.
Her foot that went the weary household round
    Dances with lightsome trip some smooth green lawn,
Her eyes, that some new duty ever found
    Waiting close by—to fairer sights are drawn,
Roses that shower pink snows through golden air,
And bowers of greenery stetching far and fair.

The lines of care engraven round her mouth
    Relax and fainter grow; the toil-worn hands
Fall in her lap—some charm-wind from the south
    Enchains her soul with fragrant flowery bands.
Her cheeks take on the soft and peachy glow
That lured the first kiss years and years ago.

And she will wake and cradle you to rest
    With merry patience—sing sweet lullabies,
And soft as down will pillow you her breast,
    And down upon you beam her love-lit eyes;
But let her sleep this little while, and bring
Back from her dreams a heart aglow with spring.

A GREEK BOY.

(Suggested by a Picture).

A tawny hide hangs o'er the shoulders fine;
    Dark, daring eyes, smile out most luringly;
Curls, where the sun-gleams linger, loving cling
    Thick round a spacious brow. By the blue sea
Thousands of years ago he roamed; what joy
    To have kept step with him along the shore;
Tended on some green turf with him the flock
    Soft-bleating—in our ears the ocean's roar!
That hand, methinks, would ply the oar with ease,
    The cheek has that warm tint burnt by the sun;
No maidish youth was he in love or sports,
    Swifter than Mercury's his feet could run:
Beauty, but 'tis the rock-born eagle's grace.
    The witchery of this face appeals to me,
Over the tide of years that soundless flow
    Because this soul would die for liberty.

AN ETCHING.

Within my mind a faint grey seascape grows,
    And I must paint it—bring from out the brain
Its shadowy outlines, make it fast with words,
    Or it will flee and never come again.
A West wind blows. Out on the distant tide
    A few white sails gleam silvery in the sun;
Deep purple is the sea at furthest rim,
    Whilst on the lower sands the waves break dun.
High, dry on shingly beach the boats are pulled,
    Waiting till sturdy fishers row far out
Under the midnight stars, whilst dear ones wait
    Their safe return with many an ache of doubt.
How still, how tranquil, is the quaint, small town!
    Its windmill's sails go slowly round and round;
The little houses bathed in sunshine stand,
    And flowers blow in plots of garden ground.
Nothing is heard but cry of wandering bird,
    And buzz of turning sails blown by the wind.
The morning stirs with its light breath grey grass
    Close to the sea, which oft the billows find.

A WINTER'S SCENE.

A white world, with a spectral sun that hangs
    In ash-grey sky—the leafless trees are full
Of soft, pure balls that one could almost think,
    (So fair and white they are) were fairy wool.
The ugly houses wear a bridal look,
    And gardens all are snugly covered up;
But underneath that cloak what charms are hid!
    Purple and gold in many a fragrant cup.
The speckled throstle picks amongst the snow
    For crumbs that may be hidden—folds his wing,
And shivers as he looks with hungry eye,
    And yearns to hear the step of laughing Spring.

THE WORLD.

Thinking of places sweet and green beneath the spreading sky
I almost breathe the pagan prayer that I might never die.
Looking upon the rising sun I wish to watch him rise for aye,
And night is fair with candle-light, and all the music of the day.

But thinking if my prayer was heard, lengthened my mortal years,
Why, if the smiles were multiplied, so also were the tears,
And spots most beautiful would seem like grave-yards dank and
    drear.
If we must move 'midst faces strange that knew us not in yester year.

The trees are fair because we sat under their boughs in summer heat,
And there is more than mortal charm that makes us love this
    window seat,
For here we watched the harvest moon scud from beneath a bank
    of cloud
And by its light each other saw, and felt the heart beat fast and loud.

When they are gone we loved so well, like aliens roam we through
    the earth,
And jangled out of harmony are all familiar sounds of mirth;
The spell that binds us to the earth is snapped asunder—let us go!
For not for us the sun, moon, and stars—nor moorland breezes
    glorious blow.

THE UNIVERSAL LIFE.

Wide open stands the door of my soul
    And the world's men and women troop through;
Some weeping, some laughing, some dumb with despair,
    Wearing roses, and fennel, and rue;
And the beat of their feet makes a martial refrain—
    Come in, I am waiting for you.

Wide open stands the door of my soul,
    And the victor and vanquished tramp in;
Come the makers of music immortal and sweet,
    Come the stirrers of conflict and din;
And their voices sound loud as the roar of the sea—
    O voices, I bid you come in.

Wide open stands the door of my soul,
    And the noble, the brave, the soul-freed
Come wearing the palm that they won with their pain,
    Come the puny souls fettered with greed;
And I greet with my best love the soul of the serf,
    Which the valiant and pure cannot need.

Wide open stands the door of my soul,
    And the lover and loved one stand there.
I am glad that the lover is tender and true,
    That the loved one is blooming and fair;
But the best place I keep for the soul that waits lone,
    As one tree in the forest stands bare.

Wide open stands the door of my soul,
    Comes the mother, soft hushing her child;
Babbling stories unnumbered of baby tricks done.
    Of the times it has whimpered or smiled—
But I lock my arms close round the great mother-soul,
    Empty-bosomed, with eyes yearning wild.

I cannot shut the door of my soul;
    Through the day and the night they pour through.
O women and men, I can ne'er sit alone,
    For my fate is all mixed up with you:
I must laugh to the end with the young and the gay—
    I must sigh with the wearers of rue.

LOVE'S GARDEN.

Somewhere, or East or West it lies,
    A garden beautiful to see;
Somewhere beneath the wide-furled skies
    Its rich flowers bloom perpetually,
Carnations redder than heart-blood,
The lily with her fair, white hood,
And scented things that have no name,
With tulips leaping into flame.

A tree stands in one corner sweet
    Wherein a magic bird doth sing,
Whilst to the rhythm of bright feet
    A sunlit fountain swift doth spring.
Who opes the gate and enters there
Must ever nurse a fragrant care;
Nor ever more can wander free
By lake and river, glade and sea.

Yet, say the chroniclers of old,
    Thousands for entrance search and sigh;
Their liberty seems bleak and cold,
    They offer it these sweets to buy.
Then once within some fain would out,
But blunder on in paths of doubt—
If they escape 'tis but to find
They left the merry heart behind.

Somewhere, or North or South it lies,
    And casts its fragrance on the breeze;
Violets more dark than houris' eyes
    Grow in the shadow of its trees.
Some find it early, others late,
Some are misled by taunting fate,
But ever, always night and day,
Pilgrims to find it make their way.

FRIENDSHIP.

I ask thee not to share, O friend, with me
Thy sun, thy roses, youth's wild ecstasy;
    But should thy heart grow tired in future years,
    Beneath a carking load of grief and fears,
Come then, and I will sit and weep with thee.

I ask thee not to come when skies are fair,
Nor shed for me one joy-leaf from thy hair;
    But when the flowers are broken by the blast,
    The lilies rotting, roses fading fast,
Remember that I wait thy woe to share.

Sit in my heart and shelter from the rain!
Then when the sky blows blue and fair again
    I'll let thee flutter out from me once more,
    With gladness piercing to my heart's deep core,
That I was blessed to soothe thee in thy pain.

For Friendship keeps—locked in her limpid eyes—
Eternal sunbeams, never-changing skies;
    And loves us for our frailties as our worth:
    And from the very moment of her birth
Grows strong though feeding but on Sorrow's sighs.

JUNE.

With dress of forest green, and wreath both white and red,
    I saw her dance along the ways and pipe a merry tune:
Her lips, that were more soft and sweet than roses on her head,
    Were pressed close to a fresh-plucked reed, and sang the song of
    June.

She waved her wondrous wand, and earth turned blue and gold,
    This middle daughter of the year, and fairest of them all,
Who brings the reign of roses full, the bird songs new and old,
    The sigh of leaves in whose green courts the summer birds loud
    call.

How kind to wanderers lone who sleep beneath the stars!
    Their wayside couch is sudden turned to that might hold a king;
The soft grass makes a pillow cool—nothing there is that mars—
    And through their dreams there comes a sense of full leaves
    murmuring.

No longer does their plight seem beggarly and drear;
    The big white stars their candles are, and green curtains round
    are drawn;
    The wide earth is their dream-chamber, and music sweetly clear,
The birds sing in the boughs of June to tell them it is dawn.

SWEETS.

A blow of summer roses in the hedge,
  Some pink, some purely white;
And through the green below, a chuckling brook
  Reflects the sunny light.

Two maidens telling secrets in the dusk,
  And vowing friendship long;
And o'er the floor the fire flings blood-red light,
  Whilst ghostly shadows throng.

A mother seated in the meadow grass
  A laughing child beside,
Both weaving daisy-chains, whilst overhead
  The milk-white cloudlets ride.

Two lovers whispering tales of deathless love
  In a still, twilit lane;
To live, they say, with bright and faithful eyes,
  Through time, and grief, and pain.

0 sweets that come and go like gracious doves
  In the fair summer time,
We hold ye in the memory of our hearts
  Untouched by winter's rime!

When whistling winds lament o'er woodlands bare,
  And gardens heaped with snow,
The happy mind can see in dreamy mood
  A million roses blow.

THE CIRCLE.

Around the hearth-stone of the heart
    There is not room for all the world:
Some cherished few sit closely drawn,
    Warmed at Love's fire when storms are hurled.
We make the circle wider yet
    For passing guest right merrily,
But when the doors behind him close
    The circle still is two or three.

Sometimes, aflush with youth and hope,
    Upon the wings of strong delight
We strive to take the whole world in,
    But fail ere we have done it quite.
The elfin moment will not stay,
    Upon the spirit shuts the stone,
Leaving the world outside once more—
    We with our loved ones sit alone.

The heart is small, the world is wide,
    And so within the human breast
Some little spot where we were bred,
    Or north, or south, or east, or west,
Around our roots yet hangs its soil;
    And when we cross Death's chiller foam
Methinks the sweetest thing were this—
    An angel with a face from home.

EARTH'S SONG TO HER CHILDREN.

The earth is weary waiting you, 0 people!
    She yearns to hold you in her glad, green arms;
Each morning as the sun lights up the valley
    She tries to lure you with her hundred charms.
And sadly sighs, " Why do you stay away, Love,
    Why do you timorous wear those self-forged chains?
Cannot the blackbird's magic music reach you,
    Who calls, and calls, and calls in rose-starred lanes?

" The water-lily holds the sunbeam for you,
    And wonders why you never come to look;
The river glides or rushes to the ocean,
    And under drooping willows runs the brook.
All things fulfil their mission, and are joyful,
    Why do you stay so long, 0 Love of mine?
Waiting for you, I deck myself in beauty,
    Of sward and fern, gay flowers, and stately pine.

" 0 break your chains and come, for years are fleeting!
    These flowers I wear are for your absent eyes,
Soon it will be too late, dust will have filled, dear,
    Your sight, and all in vain will shout the skies.
These waves of shade that wander o'er the cornfields,
    These bursts of sun, and cool clouds scattering rain,
Cornflowers, convolvulus with silver trumpets,
    Birds singing mad, will come, O, ne'er again!

" Others like to them may troop forth, for others—
    But you may never see them, 0 come now!
Now, whilst the sun is shining on the meadows,
    And let me send the hard lines from your brow.
A long, long rest would follow, I would give you
    Sweet joy and beauty ere Life's gem be lost.
Your mother calls her truants to her bosom,
    0 come and claim her what may be the cost.

" I pour, and pour, and pour my glorious treasures
    That you may live and laugh, nor be a slave;
They come and lay you dead before your time, dear,
    And rend my breast to make your early grave.
Up like the sun, my boys, in morning's splendour,
    Smiting aside the gloomy clouds' array:
Tell them the dreary hours of night are over,
    You come to claim your mother and the day."

A MARCHING TUNE.

O, the beat of the drums,
　　And the sheen of the spears,
And red banners that toss like the sea,
　　Better far than the peace
　　That is fraught with deep death
To the wild rebel soul set in me:
Better pour out the blood in a swift crimson flood,
　　As to music we march to the grave,
Than to feel day by day the slow drops ebb away
　　From the chain-bitten heart of a slave.

O, to fight to the death,
　　With a hope through the strife
That the freedom we seek shall be ours,
　　Better far than despair
　　And the coward's weak words
Trembling back from the front of the Powers.
Better do, dare, and fail, than shake like a leaf pale
　　In the breath of the wild autumn wind:
Better death on the field with an honour bright shield
　　Than the soft bed that coward souls find.

O, we leave hearth-stone warm
　　For the rain-beaten roads,
And our arrows are hung at our sides:
　　Freedom dearer to us
　　Than the home that we leave,
Or the warm, clinging arms of the bride.
For our children's fair eyes, like the blue of the skies,
　　Foemen's gleaming with hate, chill as steel;
For the Mother-love touch that which smites over-much
　　Till the life, stricken deep, earthward reels.

We have waited so long
　　We can wait now no more,
And we march forth, our Freedom to meet;
　　Keeping step to a tune
　　That is brave as our hearts,
Whilst the stones clatter loud to our feet.
Can we fail when we fight for the sake of the light
　　From the hearths where our cradles have stood?
For the fathers long dead, for the races ahead
　　That shall spring up like flowers from our blood?

GOOD HOPE.

O weary hearts that languish for the light,
    And souls grown pale and shrunk 'neath slavish woes,
Hurried so swiftly on to death's dark brink,
    Ye scarce have time to stay and pluck life's rose!
Out of this cloud-like misery of yours,
    Beneath the shower of your fast-falling tears,
The young May-buds of Freedom shall be born,
    To crown with deathless bloom the noble, unborn years.

I dreamt the thunder-drops did patter thick
    Through the old pear-tree boughs in storm last night,
Yet there the merry birds will sit and sing,
    Sun-circled, on the bough grown full and white;
And not one sigh which leaves your pallid lips,
    One stifled sob which tyranny doth wring,
But soar, accusing angels, to the Heavens—
    Bring near and yet more near fair Freedom's balmy Spring.

LONDON.

Dearer than woods, bursting to new, bright green,
   Where whistling blackbirds shrill 'mid rose-starred briars;
Trails of white-petalled strawberries, April-washed,
   Are these grey streets, vast crowds, and silvery spires:
Wide lawns of fair loveliness, where Dawn
   Trips, leaving diamond traces of her feet:
And bramble bushes hung with gossamers
   Wake not within my heart a thrill so sweet
As when surrounded by this mighty throng,
   These varying streams of great humanity,
Bearing their little toll of flowers or weeds
   To the vast ocean of Eternity.
List to this murmur that doth rise and fall
   Like surge of billows—richer than the notes
Of blackbird, or the cuckoo's madrigal,
   Or rapturous joy of bursting linnet-throats!
The lady's cultured accents, the hoarse call
   Of violet-sellers help to swell that sound;
The child's thin treble and the beggar's drone,
   Make up the song that floods the air around.
Dear, busy hive of warm and throbbing life,
   O! what are bees and birds, and chainless sea,
Compared with men and women? These do make
   The charm that draws one evermore to thee.

A CRYING CHILD IN LONDON.

A child who cries; a muffled, dreary tone,
    As if afraid to make too great a noise;
It may be that the grief was lightly drawn,
    Some trifling wrangle over stolen toys:
Yet seemed it over-quiet for a child,
    The tears like drops of sap from some old tree
    Well slowly, and seem born with direst pain,
    Yet none did stay to wipe them tenderly.
Flower-hawkers call in voices high and shrill
    Their violets that sweet fill the gazer's mind,
With vistas of green woods, where willow-wrens
    Sing in the high tree-tops bent by the wind,
And budding as light April rain is dried
    By smiles as sudden as her clouded brow:
Whereas 'tis autumn, and the leaves fall fast,
    And London's ceaseless traffic rumbles low.
A few half-turn, then hurry swift along;
    London has bread to earn, and wealth to pour,
Prayers to be muttered, lies to sell as truths,
    And like an ocean sends her mighty roar
Of sound throughout the world—she has not time
    To stay a weeping mite and dry its tears;
Like a tired jade she bustles ever on,
    Striving to mitigate her vast arrears.

FACES THROUGH THE MIST.

Out of the wintry mist they stole,
    Weird faces framed by silvery gray;
Some by the street-lamp's yellow flame
    Gleamed sweet and fresh as flowers of May—
With lovers walking by their side,
    Who came the closer that they know
The veil that hid the moon and stars,
    And all sweet things, hid lovers, too.

Two went with light and eager steps,
    Their hearts beat warm with love and mirth,
Thinking that if they willed it so
    They might drag heaven down to earth.
Though millions failed yet would they win—
    So whispered they as on they passed;
It seemed as through the sea of mist
    A ship went by with fairy mast.

With silken sails where laughing winds
    Sang merry measures high and low,
Laden with scents as sweet as those
    That went from Eden long ago.
My blessing in its flower-wreathed prow
    Lodged; through the mist it passed once more
And may it reach the visioned port,
    Nor rock its graceful timbers gore.

Some with bent heads and heavier tread,
    And cynic lips for long unkissed,
Went by; grey faces that some fay
    Might e'en have woven from the mist;
Who long have heaved from out their bark
    Hopes, dreams, caresses unfulfilled!
Whose spices, sweets from Love's bright isle
    Into the sullen seas were spilled.

A whistling boy, his hands deep pushed
    In pockets knowing not a coin;
He chirps as blackbirds do in spring,
    Rich with the wealth none can purloin—
The branches of his soul so green,
    So full of song in wild woods fair,
He does not care one finger's snap
    For biting frost, mist-shrouded air.

The clear notes pass, as all things do,
    To silence, in the fog's grey cloak;
The shining pavements dimly show
    The amber lamp-stars. On they walk,
The young, the old, the gay, the tired,
    The whistling boy with pursed red lips;
The lovers glad. All pass away—
    The mean, small boats—the stately ships!

A YEAR'S DREAM.

Since the Christmas bells last rung
    We have woven many a dream,
Time, the tyrant harsh, has flung
    Headlong in his hurrying stream.
Never care, O, never care!
    We will weave them yet more true,
Brighter, sweeter, yet more rare—
    Laughing, singing—I and you.

Since the carollers sang clear
    Resolutions fine and pure,
As the snow-men we did rear
    Long ago, could not endure.
What's the good of weeping then?
    As the sunshine melts the snow,
Resolutions, like white men,
    Come to nothing: sing " Heigho! "

Yet keep building, dreaming on;
    Better that than sleep—despair;
And perchance, when we are gone,
    Some slight fragment, sweet and fair,
Of our dreams and buildings long
    May a little time remain;
Better striving, laughter, song,
    Than the sluggard's poppied gain.

They who never weave a dream
    Never know the colours dear;
Always walking by life's stream
    With bent heads from year to year.
(As the patient horses do,
    Pulling boats whilst others ride);
Never see the sky of blue,
    Nor the grasses by the side.

These are they who make our chains
    Keep their strength. Oh, let us dream
Of a world where Beauty reigns,
    And a nobler, wider stream—
Till from all that men have built,
    Produce of their smiles and tears,
All the blood that they have spilt,
    Men unborn make happier years.

A FRIEND LOST.

My friend sailed out across the ocean tide,
    Who oft had sung, laughed, told us tales self-spun;
It seemed to us at first he almost died,
    Or as a cloud had covered up the sun.
No more beside the waning fire we sat,
    A charmed circle, hanging on his words,
Or lightly ran to greet his loud rat-tat,
    A sudden silence froze sweet Friendship's chords.
But now a spirit friend is everywhere,
    Smiles on us from the room with fire glow red,
Sits at the table, takes the vacant chair,
    And grows in stature higher by a head.
Brings distant cities near, and heaving seas,
    Speeds o'er the Atlantic waves, sun, cloud, and breeze.

BEYOND.

Beyond! Let us not question, thou and I,
About the world that in such mist doth lie,
The searches of the greatest and most wise
Have found it not—turn we our longing eyes
Back unto this—illumed through sorrow's tears
With hope's fresh sunbeams; tear-drops for the years
That we have squandered in our searchings vain—
Smiles,—that we find our long-lost heaven again!

Beyond! beyond! the hiding mist hangs low
Across the sea. Our dear ones long ago
Set out from us and braved the blustering gale;
Awhile we stood and watched their glimmering sail
Fade into distance—for their joyful shout
We waited—waited! Then came ache of doubt,
For silence, heavy as a frozen sea,
Returned to greet us from Eternity.

So that we only feel the hands we clasp
May melt like sun-warmed snow-drifts from our grasp;
And clasp them tighter—harsh words no more fling
Against the weaker ones. Will they not bring
Dark floods of sorrow when they sail beyond
The reach of all our sweetest words and fond?
We only strive to bring the irised glow
Of Paradise into this world we know.

And couched on the moorland's purple breast
Whilst overhead the lapwing guards her nest
With shrilly call—and blue hills gently rise
Around us—seeming touch the leaning skies,
Which like faint azure curtains o'er are drawn,
Or watch the glorious coming of the dawn,
We smile to think of all our ache and fear
And search for heaven—which waiteth for us here.

OUR HOUSEHOLD GODS.

A strangely human look our gods take on
    From living with us through the changeful years:
We gaze, and see no lifeless soulless things,
    But spirits, bearing prints of smiles and tears.
The kettle, singing gaily on the hob,
    Has taken on twice o'er a sombre note—
As in the darkened house sat funeral guests
    We heard the anguish hissing in its throat.

And it has whistled blithe on frosty nights
    Shouting impatiently, " I wait! I wait! "
When we have laughed with sweet friends round the fire,
    Forgetting that the hour was growing late.
This creaking chair would scarce a florin bring,
    To much light laughter knocked down at a sale;
I think of dear ones who have rested there—
    And swear 'tis priceless, lips unsteady, pale.

The terraced houses with their windows high,
    Their corniced ceilings, oak stairs, frescoed halls,
Would leave my heart all homesick for the glint
    Of firelight in dark nooks and o'er loved walls.
The hearth-stone shrine where we have gathered close
    When bleak winds wailed and raved across the moor—
Where those behind now talk of those away
    As of past riches, men forlorn and poor.

To thee, the stranger, sitting for a space
    Within my house, these god-souls will not speak;
Unconscious of the spirits hidden there,
    And smiling as the quaint old chair doth creak;
Thou seest no shadows entering at the door,
    No songs call to thee from this fire of mine—
But sit in thine own house, calm, still, at eve,
    And thine own gods will make thy heart a shrine.

THE HOME VOICE.

A whispering voice that comes when shadows fall,
    And evening winds are shivering spectral pines;
When mothers by the mill-stream send the cry
    That calls to where the bed-time lantern shines.
All through the day I stay my listening ears,
    But when the mothers call their children home,
Sending their voices 'cross the darkening stream,
    I hear that song o'er leagues of whitening foam.

Not mountains clothed with pines 'gainst bluest skies—
    With snowy hollow silent to the brim,
Nor forest aisles of splendid gloom and glow
    Wherein the mating birds chant joyous hymn—
Not all the things of new and sweet and strange,
    Wherewith heaped full my day heart loves to roam,
Can mute my ears against that evening cry
    When mothers call, " 'Tis bed-time! Come ye home! "

FORGOTTEN DAYS.

Whence come these memories telling me
    Of glorious lives I've lived before?
Whence float those pictures of strange lands,
    And sound of sea from unseen shore?
The salt spray flying 'gainst my cheek
Blown from a laughing, dimpling creek,
Wakes tears that come I know not why
If not for sea-years drifted by.

The sun who sets 'midst gorgeous flakes
    Of purples deep, and amber glows,
With faded greens and coolest greys,
    And spurts as red as reddest rose,
It seems to me has shed its rays
Upon me in forgotten days
When, maybe, curfews slowly tolled,
And earth was centuries less old.

These friends that take me by the hand
    Come to me with familiar grace;
It sometimes seems to me I've met
    Them in the past: each frank, free face
Brings me such pleasure that I know
I must have loved them long ago—
Have looked deep down into their eyes,
And with them watched the great sun rise.

IMMORTALITY.

In a hundred years or more Spring will come with her garlands of bloom,
And her new lovers walk in the sun when her old lovers rest in the tomb;
Whilst for us golden rains drip unheard and the warm sunlight burns
    all unseen,
And the lilac spray waves in the wind, and the wren takes her mate in
    the green;
And we sleep well and long underground, and have done with the
    laughter and tears,
Who are building to-day the fair world that shall be in a hundred years.

In a hundred years or more they will sing sweeter songs than we know,
And the rain that is falling on us will have helped their red roses to grow;
And we never may hark to the gladness that throbs through the chaos
    of pain,
That we bore unto them through the darkness, the raging of wind and
    of rain ,
But the music shall echo for all time that grew from our striving and
    tears,
And shall ring down the ages with joy unto men in a hundred years.

The best thoughts we are thinking to-day shall be living and active
    and strong,
When we sleep at the end of the fight, caring not for the war-whoop or
    song,
And it matters far more than we know that we keep our hearts
    steadfast and brave,
For the strength that they held shall walk forth when they mix with
    the dust of the grave,
And immortal, and lovely, and young shall our dream live unclouded
    by tears,
When we take the long rest that is sweet after toil in a hundred years.

LOOKING BACK.

When we look back after the battle-smoke
   Has cleared away, oft where we think we lost,
We shall behold that it was victory,
   Knowing the banners which to earth were tossed
Shall stream again before the merry wind
   With brave hearts following on for evermore—
That men fail only when they die for naught,
   Not when they win one step towards the shore.

When we look back, fast nearing the long rest—
   The bed that waits to hold each weary limb—
What do you think the sweetest thing will be
   To lie remembering when the eyes grow dim?
Not that we hoarded up excess of wealth,
   Nor e'en of lovely places where we roved,
But that through all the tricks of chance and time,
   From starting on the path, we have been loved.

'Twill not be hard to follow where they went;
   The nearing wave may take us where it list,
So that it brings us nearer to the hands
   We held awhile in ours—the lips we kissed:
As for the world we leave, it will go on—
   For lovers and the ones beloved a heaven!
And we have done our duty well if we
   Ourselves and those who follow us have given.

We cannot now disparage this dear world,
   Its stars and sun-sheen, flowers, fern-fronds and briars,
Because we follow outward with the tide
   To lands unknown; its yearnings, mad desires,
Its music, discords, tears, and laughter light
   Were sweet to us and bind us even yet;
A fair brave life! One glistening hour of it
   Was worth ten years with grief-brine grey and wet!

FAITH.

Most earnestly and truly I believe
    The human heart is beautiful and good:
Though poisonous weeds upgrow within its clefts
    As nightshade grows within the verdant wood.
There are soft streams that flow with gentle sound,
    And pearly sprays of blossom—and the grove
Is flooded with the music of sweet birds—
    So o'er its dark emotions triumphs love.
Let me keep clear unto the end of life
    My faith in sweet humanity's fair flower;
Old age, that sits with all its glamour gone,
    Cynical, cold, and infidel and sour
Is something to be shrunk from, but the light
    Of youth's departed glory hovers still
About the one who keeps through winter's rime,
    The thought that hearts are good and seldom ill.
Yet will I trust, for better 'tis to fall
    Through trusting much than trusting not at all.

POSSESSION.

There bloomed by my cottage door
    A rose with a heart scented sweet
O so lovely and fair, that I plucked it one day;
    Laid it over my own heart's quick beat.
In a moment its petals were shed,
    Just a tiny white mound at my feet.

There flew through my casement low
    A linnet who richly could sing;
Sang so thrillingly sweet I could not let it go,
    But must cage it, the glad, pretty thing,
But it died in the cage I had made,
    Not a note to my chamber would bring.

There came to my lonely soul
    A friend I had waited for long;
And the deep chilly silence lay stricken and dead
    Pierced to death by our love and our song.
And I thought on the bird and the flower,
    And my soul in its knowledge grew strong.

Go out when thou wilt, O friend—
    Sing thy song, roam the world glad and free;
By the holding I lose, by the giving I gain,
    And the gods cannot take thee from me;
For a song and a scent on the wind
    Shall drift in through the doorway from thee.

LIFE.

Life was made for joy, not woe—
    Whatever saints may say;
We were not meant, with heads bent low,
    To walk a briary way.
'Twas man transposed to minor strain
    Life's page of love and laughter;
Someday we'll change it back again,
    Whate'er may follow after.

O, Life was made for love, not hate—
    Whatever warriors say;
And Love will rule or soon or late,
    With Freedom's fragrant May.
Life's page was meant for joy's rich bloom,
    For sunlight, roses, laughter—
Between the cradle and the tomb,
    Whate'er may follow after.

FREEDOM.

Freedom comes slowly, but remember she
    Must beg from door to door, a barefoot maid;
No high-born dome in gilded car she rides.
    Full oft beneath the stars her bed is made,
And men repulse her often. Yet her eyes
    Rain drops of purest pity; as for hate,
It finds no entrance to her noble heart,
    And she will bless the toiler soon or late.

The thorns along the path of centuries
    Have deeply scarred her delicate brown feet;
Her gown is torn by many a thicket wild
    Which she has wandered through; her broad brow sweet
Is crowned by fadeless roses lovers placed
    To cheer her heart as on her way she came;
Her flesh oft faints beside the roadside hard.
    Her spirit cannot die—'tis made of flame.

A FUTURE CRADLE SONG.

Child of love and joy and hope,
    Sleep awhile, for nightfall comes;
All the birds are fast asleep,
    In their leafy, whispering homes.
Sleep, that thou mayst grow full strong
    For the work that is delight,
For the glory of the noon,
    For the peace and charm of night.
For the tossing of the sea,
    Mountain passes darkly wild—
All the world here waits for thee,
    Sleep, grow strong, our little child.
Face of sun, and moon and stars,
    Moorlands ragged, mountain stairs,
Morning mists and sunset's pomps,
    Love of woman, noble cares—
Shall be thine when thou art strong,
    Sleep, till day brings light and song.

IN FARNHAM PARK.

(Dedicated to Miss Gertrude Robertson.)

If suddenly should burst upon the sight
   Through droopings of these boughs so coolly green
Diana with white horn—with sweet delight
   Without surprise, the eye would view the scene;
For here are spaces wide, with dim oak shade,
As fair as those where she so often strayed.

The sound of the world's rush is scarcely heard—
   Anon the ear may catch the mellow bell,
Chiming through full-leaved bowers—or call of bird—
   Notes that but deeper make the aerial spell:
And when the sun makes golden ways, the grass
Seems waiting for the nymphs that used to pass,

In days of old, when man had time to dream,
   And life moved with a nobler pulse, if slow;
And there were fairies hid in every stream
   That laved the pulpy rushes—long ago!
Alas! dear days, and will ye not return?
Swift turning, hot and tired, the world doth yearn.

Such drooping of full branches that appear
   Just touched by Autumn's finger, and turned pale,
A few, for fear of all their doom, shown clear,
   To whirl and dance in death upon the gale!
Such caw of rooks and rustling leaves of trees
Conspiring with the early morning breeze.

And blue, blue shadows changing like the sea,
   Where now and then a playful sunbeam flits
Like a gold sail, whilst swooping mournfully
   To earth a faded leaf all lonesome sits;
Again the silvery bell calls through the green,
And so farewell unto the sylvan scene.

FAILURE.

THE arrows that he shot fell back to earth,
  The seed he scattered fell, yet bore no flowers;
Men made his name a little butt for mirth,
  Till even Hope fled from the ruined bowers:
Yet, hopeless of success, he still fought on
Till day's bright reign was o'er and life was done.

He looked along the grey and flinty way,
  Roseless and lightened with no joyous beam;
He saw again the youth so brave and gay,
  Who brightened all things with his radiant dream—
I fought, he said, and not one lie fell slain;
I sowed—no flower sprang up 'neath sun and rain.

Some with their laugh won more than all my tears;
  They danced along the path I climbed so slow,
And reaped the harvest in the early years,
  And stood on high tops near the sun's warm glow—
Yet though I won it not with labours long,
My soul knows that it well deserved the song.

I envy not the laurel—it is theirs:
  Those born 'neath happier stars, close to their time;
Envy has touched me not, if gaunt despairs,
  Nor cast upon my heart its bittering rime.
If I won not, 'twas for no sluggard sleep,
Nor for the lack of true courageous leap.

So keep your laurels—write my name with those
  Who nobly failed where some ignobly won:
Perchance some glory round about them glows
  That takes its splendour from the tireless sun.
Write thus: He fought from daylight to the dark,
And every arrow bounded from its mark.

And yet this rest will be a warrior's rest
  As hardly earned as those who won the field;
For from the star-wane to the reddening west
  The heart that conquered not would never yield.
Write failure if you will. Those who fight on
When hope has flown are close to Victory's sun.

AFTERWORD.

I HAVE given my best, I have gathered each thought
From my heart's changing garden, and to you have brought;
You may praise, you may scorn, but my spirit has rest
In the arms of this thought—" I have given my best."
I have given my best. Though the poor flowers I bring
Be not lilies nor roses, but just such as spring
In the cool, quiet hedgerow, to catch the tired eye
Of the labourer going homewards 'neath even's grey sky:
He may crush with his heel, he may warm with his breast—
It is all one to me—I have given my best.

VOICES OF WOMANHOOD

To Mr. W. H. BURNETT,EDITOR OF LATE "BLACKBURN
STANDARD AND EXPRESS," AND ONE TIME PRESIDENT OF
BLACKBURN AUTHORS' ASSOCIATION, I DEDICATE THIS
BOOK, AS A SMALL TOKEN OF AFFECTION AND ESTEEM,
AND GRATEFUL REMEMBRANCE OF HIS BEING MY FIRST
LITERARY FRIEND, AND FOR HIS FIRST INTRODUCING ME
TO THE READING PUBLIC.

April, 1914.

For permission to reprint "A Fireside Fancy" and "The Second
Mother" I am indebted to the kindness of Messrs. Partridge,
and the Editor of the "Children's Friend" and " Family Friend."

CONTENTS

PRELUDE

Voices impetuous, daring, and wild;
    Voices of agony, moaning, and fear;
Voices of yearning, with sorrowful sigh,
    These through the silence I listen, and hear.
Whispers that faint in the great world of sound,
    Echoes that linger a moment—to die!
Murmurs of tenderness over the cot,
    Murmurs of weariness for the wide sky.
Out of the mystical silence they float,
    Voices of rebel, or motherhood mild;
Love to you, gentle ones, crowned with white peace.
    Voices impetuous, daring and wild,
What shall we give to ye, blazing new trails?
    Prison, and scorning, loud laughter and jeers,
These give they all those who seek for new lands!
    What shall a poet give? Shall it be tears?
I, as you pass, unashamed, unafraid,
    Out from the silence to cry against wrong
Wave Song's bright banner, and smile that the world
    Yet has its heroes so splendidly strong.

LIFE.

Let me know all, Life, all!
    The pain, the gloom, the strife,
The height, the depth, the fall—
    I only ask for Life.

Give me no sheltering wings
    To shield me from distress,
Of great and tiny things,
    Life! Life! I ask no less.

For when it all is done,
    All suffered and all known,
Lightning and rain and sun—
    There's time to be a stone.

A stone to lie quite still,
    Without a single care,
Without a need to fill,
    Without a joy to share!

Save me from those who shield
    From danger and from doom.
Give me the open field,
    No risk is but—a tomb.

A REBEL SONG.

Be not afraid, whate'er they say,
    Tyrant and priest, and threatening gun!
Thy father for one inch of way
    Died—with his face towards the sun.

Fear not their chains, my little child,
    None are so vile and strong as fear;
Hope guards the prisoned eagle wild,
    Truth's voice from living tombs speaks clear.

The vultures on the lion feed!
    But let this be thine inmost stay:
There's heaven in hell for those who bleed
    To win an inch of Freedom's way.

WHY?

The man is free to come and free to go,
    To earn his crust, and bed, and journey on
And hush the restless cry that's in his blood,
    But I must hear it plead till life is done.

He sleeps in forest leaves so fresh and brown,
    He drinks from the cold spring that tastes of earth,
And looks in eyes of men with hearts akin—
    But I must stay pot-bound in place of birth.

My limbs are strong to toil from morn to night,
    Or waste in dungeons dark for Freedom's sake,
And throats as soft and white the rope has stung,
    And hearts as womanly the fool may break.

I'm strong for labour, pain, and heat of day,
    My little hands may fight the vile disease;
And through the darkened vale I bring back life,
    And choose the hardship rather than the ease.

The heart that's bold within the narrow room
    Is fit for outside chance and mountain climb,
And open doors that lead us God knows where—
    And will not shut until the end of Time.

A WISH.

When I must pass from out this mortal life,
Lay down for evermore its joy and strife,
    O, may the one who lifts my sinking head
    Be not such as sees goodness in the dead,
And stabs the living like a poisoned knife;

Nor one to weep and pray, and paint for me
The glory of the life that is to be;
    But rather one to speak of joys gone by,
    Till sleep comes softly down upon mine eye,
And sense is lost in Time's infinity.

No solemn, dark-cowled priest drone at mine ear,
But someone that I love in accents clear
    Sing an old song we learnt when gay and young,
    When o'er our heads the bursting blossoms hung,
And I shall pass away without a fear.

Nor let the dismal shadows of the tomb
Like a black raven's wing make dark each room.
    Through unveiled windows let the glorious light
    Stream in unchecked. I ever held it right
To give this o'er-sad world no tithe of gloom.

AUTUMN.

When autumn days are come at last,
And lengthening shades are closing fast,
When wild wet winds sigh out their grief,
And all the woods are red of leaf,
May all my toil in sun and rain
Yield me, before I turn again,
One tranquil hour of rest before
I, silent, pass and close the door.

I would not pass in act of toil,
But sheathe my spade within the soil,
And look around on field and sky
As one who stays to say good-bye,
And see the folk who ploughed with me,
And guess at furrows yet to be,

And know, though fields are grey with cloud,
That Spring will come with sun-shafts proud.
I would not hurry swift away
As careless, thoughtless hirelings may,
But, dignified, would rest before
I, silent, pass and close the door.

A VISION.[1]

There is a silent woman in this land—
A silent woman, thinking all this while
Beside a fire upon a little hearth
As narrow as a cradle—or a grave!
Strange echoes reach her from the world outside,
And move, and thrill her; but she sits and waits
And muses in her corner 'midst the shades.
She listens to the voices from her hearth,
And answers not again nor contradicts.
Though sometimes in her eyes a smile will gleam,
A shadow sometimes rest upon her brow.
And all this while she never speaks a word
Save gentle love. And by her house there sound
A thousand echoes from the world outside.
When she shall speak, ah, then the world will hear,
Will listen as she listened all this while,
For as her strength was in the little house
So strong will be her presence in the world.

---

1   By kind permission of *The Daily Herald*

THE CRADLE.

This cradle was an acorn once;
    The great winds rocked it with a song
Through sunny noons and starry nights,
    And bade it grow both fair and strong.
" Oh, lullaby! " the blithe winds said
Until, quite brown and ripe, 'twas shed.

Then in the dewy dark it lay
    And missed the rocking of the wind,
And felt the fire-like shoots of life,
    And struggled through Pain's pathways blind,
Until a little leaf flashed green
And knew the sun yet cheered the scene.

Mighty and strong it grew, until,
    A well-ringed tree, 'twas felled at last.
It tottered groaning to the earth
    With thought that life was surely past—
To cradle thee, my dear delight,
Through sunny morn and starry night.

Child, grow thou as the acorn grew,
    The world is fair, say what we will,—
Growth in the darkness when we fall,
    And daring hearts may top the hill.
Oh, lullaby, sing lullaby,
The fruitful earth looks to the sky.

THE NEW COMMANDMENT.

Thou shalt not steal; nor shall one steal from thee
    Thy right to live beneath a summer sky,
To toil or play in happy liberty,
    And, when thy day is done, tranquil to die.
Respect thy brother's right, nor let thine own
    Be filched from thee—that vital, simple right
To roses, bread, and life's full undertone,
    And all the swift, high notes of sweet delight.
However honoured, ermined be the thief,
    Let him not slip away to boast the deed;
It will not boot to mourn in helpless grief,
    Or wring thine hands and say thy heart doth bleed.
Upon him, like the lightning, radiant, strong!
    Or on thy soul shall lie one half the blame,
And cowardice, with all his trembling throng,
    Shall make thy children's children curse thy name.

THE LOST COMRADE.

The toiling man who, by a whim of chance,
    Or little gift the gods gave at his birth,
Some power discovered in his own strange breast
    Whilst others gazed—unconscious of their worth;
The man who climbed, forgetful of the time
    He shared our sweat, our bread, our grinding care,
And sometimes cursed with us beneath his breath,—
    When he falls, then,— ah, what a fall is there!
Of all the lost most sadly, utterly,
    Most deeply, darkly, damnably shut out;
The greatest leader stood a world apart,
    We sometimes watched with smiling eyes of doubt.
But he, our very own—oh, grief, oh, shame!—
    When he destroys himself in us, at death
He lies without a people and a place,
    Unclassed, despised and mourned by no true breath,
Whilst outcasts of the world yet boast a race,
    Possessing nothing but our heart's warm place.

HIS BOOKS.

He loved his books. They stood there row on row,
　　Red, green, and blue, and some in twilight-grey,
And some, with gilding. I walked soft and slow.
　　I think he sat and read them night and day.
He slept the fewest hours—and how he bent!
　　A tradesman's knocking made him stir and curse,
Because, at such a sound, some great thought went.
　　He bent above his book as a tired nurse
Bends, crooning, tender, over a sick child.
　　It was the greatest task to mend his coat!
I've seen him pass into the night so wild
　　Without an umbrella—wrapped in thought;
Whilst I feared for his chest, yet dared not speak,
　　For talking-folk he hated, and I fear
He would have said a servant should be meek
　　And cold—who got her twenty pounds a year.
-His window looked upon a quiet square
　　With great trees always swaying up and down
As if they thought him foolish sitting there,
　　And asked him to come out and see the town.
Mine was a little attic, right away,
　　And all my work was o'er by candle-light,
And there I used to sit, and sew and pray.
　　Before I went to bed, yes, every night,
I crept down all those stairs—aye, seventy-four,
　　Soft, with the candle shaded by my hand,
To see that bar of light beneath his door,
　　And say good-night to it. That light was grand,—
That little lonely bar of heavenly gold
　　Escaping from the grip of the grim dark,—
And what it meant to me I scarce have told.
　　'Twas like an angel light that shone to mark
Division from his work and that of mine;
　　I never saw it but my eyes held tears,
And yet I think my sorrow was divine—
　　I served him well and faithful twenty years,
And he—he never guessed that with his bread
　　I mixed in love and sorrow, and my fear
That he'd leave off his coat—and soon be dead.
　　He never knew how much I loved his sneer,
That fine, fine sneer when visitors would call
　　And try to draw him from his peaceful den,

(And I went down and lied there in the hall)
    To waste and war and muddle up with men.
Once, only once, he seemed to note that I
    Was a fair woman, for he turned his head
A moment from his book and looked full sly,
    And said a day would come when I should wed;
But as for him, he hoped it would be late,
    For I was a good servant, quiet, staid,
And understood him and his quiet fate,
    And of his sombreness was ne'er afraid.
One night he came in with some purchased books
    And called me from the attic to his room,
And fear rushed on my spirit with his looks—
    A dampness and a terror like the tomb.
I called help in, and put him snug to bed,
    And fought with death for him, but all in vain,
For he was dying then, the doctor said,
    And all that night there fell a sighing rain.
Between his torpor he was talking soft
    Of new books that he'd bought and what they held,
And of his old ones, often, aye, so oft;
    My heart with very agony was felled.
And I—I dared not kiss him—lest he know,
    For he, he paid me twenty pounds a year
To clean, and cook, and speak in accents low,
    He never asked me for a loving tear.
And then the nurse came and she looked on me
    As if I nothing knew—and closed the door,
But I was always listening tenderly
    Until I knew that everything was o'er.
And then I got my chance. The nurse was out,
    The little room was quiet, where he lay,
And I was unafraid, and had no doubt
    Or dread of death to fill me with dismay.
So I pushed back the door and kissed his brow,
    And told him that I loved him—loved his looks,
However cold or terrible—just how
    I even loved him as he loved his books.
That was my chance. When dusting strangers' rooms
    And listening to their orders high and shrill,
Upon my world of grey a bright joy blooms—
    I took my chance and kissed him, calm and still.

And in my one lone room I have his books,
　　Bought with the hundred pounds he left to me,
And so can conjure up the master's looks,
　　The lonely square, the midnight lamp, the tea
I often took him, which he rarely drank.
　　I cannot read his books—they're mostly dry,
And leave my head a little aching blank.
　　I'll love his books and him until I die.
And so he got my service, love and tear,
　　And got it all for twenty pounds a year!

LA FEMME.

I am weak—they have sung it in song,
    For my eyes are soon melted to tears;
But the lords of the earth they are strong,
    So the annals have told us for years.
They are strong—yet my tears as they fall
    Win a way through their hearts hard as mail.
And my smile that swims through like a sun
    Shakes the soul that red war made not quail.

I am weak—they have measured my might
    By the force of my little, white hand;
But they fought, and they bled, and they died,
    When my lips breathed the word of command!
Heroes—gods—fell at Troy for my sake,
    Mauled to death by the blood-hounds of War,
Whilst I laughed with my Paris far off—
    And my beauty a bright, evil star!

They have conquered the hosts of the sea,
    But I came, and my Nelson fell down.
They have smiled at the snarl of the wolf,
    But turned pale with alarm at my frown!
Great Antonius, thirsty for power,
    Lost the world at the glance of my eye,
All the purple and pomp of its show
    As a poor, worthless clout casting by.

And the martyrs, and lovers, and kings
    I have cradled and hushed at my breast!
I have rocked the Immortals to sleep
    With an old simple rune full of rest;
And the warriors who hurled the bright spears
    On a day with my milk were content—
Alexanders who wept for two worlds,
    For a while in my lap happy went.

I am weak—I have bent my fair neck
  Where the guillotine throws its black shade,
And have walked with a proud, queenly tread,
  Dying well on the doom I have made!
I have roamed lonely fields of the slain,
  Lamp in hand, for the lover I loved—
  An Evangeline, faithful to death,
Through the dead and the dying slow moved.
  In my face are the lily and rose,

In my eyes tints of sunlight and sea,
  Whilst my voice weds all sweet notes in one;
Yet an end unto beauty must be!
  For the white winter snaps down the flower,
And the sunlight is swallowed in gloom,
  And the voice like a bell's golden chime
Cannot sound through the dust of the tomb.

Yet I walk forth again and again,
  Along highway, and byeway, and glen,
And my soul is the same evermore
  As it bursts on the rapt sight of men.
Till the last man has sung into sleep,
  All the stars fallen red from the sky,
With the last woman dead at his side
  Shall the spell I have thrown flit not by.

SONG OF THE PHARISEES.

Despise them that they could not tell
    The sweet from bitter, false from true,
Or knowing, all too weakly fell,
Cast heaven away, preferring hell,
    Not wise as I and you.

Who fluttered, fell into the flame
    That threw for us no golden lure,
Too well we recognised its shame,
And back with wings scarce heated came,
    Because we feared the more.

Who know not love, but only lust,
    The burning thorn without the rose;
Earth's beauty just a stretch of dust,
Whereon they scramble for a crust;
    The sky a thing that snows.

So wise and good, with eyesight clear,
    We sit serene in Paradise,
And pat ourselves that we are here,
With many a righteous sigh (or sneer)
    For those not half so wise.

COWARD OR FOOL.

I'd rather be the noble fool
    Who strives to win the upward track,
And dies for naught through too much haste,
    Than jolt the wheels of Progress back.

My bones, picked clean by vulture hordes,
    Whitening beneath the free sky's blue,
Should cry to every nearing foot,
    " Fear not. This is the worst they do! "

No room for cowards! but the fool
    Who fails from nobleness sublime
Shall share the wreath with those more wise,
    Who on her failures stand, and climb.

IN STORMY DAYS.

'There is a deep and sacred joy in living,
 Not only through the calm and sunny days,
But when the heart in trembling drops is giving
 Red blood-dew, as great Sorrow's pallid haze
Lies thick athwart the sighing shores of life,
And we reel back, half-fainting in the strife,

Half-beaten, till Hope comes with balm-tipped fingers,
 To send us nerved again unto the fray;
With souls in which her lightest whisper lingers,
 To rise once more unawed. Not just when May
Unfolds her snow-white banners to warm air
We say unto ourselves that life is fair.

Tho' blustering winds sink 'neath Despair's black ocean
 Our fragile dreams, with roses round each prow,
Dreams rising 'bove the heart's sad, wild emotion,
 Above the agony of the mad blow—
When tides recede we search along the shore,
Building from wrecks more nobly than before.

When through the woods we roam where, lately cooing,
 Soft doves were nesting in the branches green,
And silence echoes now the wild wind's soughing,
 We feel that, locked within the mournful scene,
Are the sweet vi'lets, that, laughing, bring
Fragrance and beauty with the birth of Spring.

A little space, defeat and dearth may crush us,
 But, buoyant, riding o'er a flood of tears,
The heart soars up; hopes once again flush o'er us;
 And, gazing with clear eyes o'er all the years,
We see that storms bring strength, and through the veins
Exquisite rapture triumphs o'er our pains.

The feet, unmoulded, that must march behind us
 We feel will stumble less that we have trod
The thorns before them; and the chains that bind us
 Do hang less heavily in that the sod
Has drunk our blood in weary marching hours,
For richly 'neath their feet shall spring the flowers.

HER SUNDAY OUT.

Dear me, but what a week it's been!
　　Duster and clout from day to day,
And calm commands and gentle hints,
　　And never once a word to say.
But as I've passed the big hall clock
　　With white moon-face and waggish tick,
I'm almost sure I saw him wink
　　To hear me say, " I'm sick, sick, sick! "

Sometimes I've nigh forgot that I
　　Am flesh and blood. Oh what a night!
I'll wear the hat with lilac flowers,
　　And my new gloves, so sweet and bright.
I wonder if he's waiting now!
　　It's precious fine to have a beau,
To hear your skirts swish over grass,
　　And know that someone waits for you.

It makes you think you are someone—
　　In spite of eating scrappy grub
Alone, as some offensive thing,
　　Then bending down to rub and scrub—
To smell the wild flowers in the hedge
　　And walk through wet and tangled green,
With someone helping you along
　　Might make you fancy you're a queen.

The self that dares not speak or laugh
　　Shall live to-night. O scented dew!
In yonder wood the cuckoo calls,
　　And glad am I his notes are few.*
And now I hear a sweeter sound,
　　A well known whistle, loud and clear!
If every night were Sunday night
　　Monday would have no cast of fear.

* Referring to the North Country superstition that as many
years must pass as the cuckoo's calls before the hearer is
married.

EPITAPH ON A TOILER'S CHILD.

Sleep, pretty one, who hast not known
The care that's heavier than a stone,
The heated rush from morn to night
Till life grows barren of delight,
The stunted soul, the wearied limb
And bright blue eyes too early dim,
The dreams too early thrust aside
To swell the merchant's worldly pride.
Thou hast not known the endless day
When every hour is wished away,
And toil and sickness, wrestling, stand—
The aching heart, the trembling hand,
That still must ply the wearying thread
To earn its dole of daily bread.
Thou hast not, quivering, felt the life
Of mother, sister, child or wife
Dependent on thy body's health,
The power that heaps thy master's wealth!
Death with a few short pangs gave rest,
He snatched thee from thy mother's breast,
And chained thee in his fetters cold,
A tyrant merciless and bold;
Yet he was generous in his power,
The agony was but an hour,
And when 'twas o'er no meaner might
Could bring a pang or mar delight.

SHAME.

Thou can forgive a man a thousand things,
The sharp word, and the scornful tyrant-glance,
The hot impatience; and your heart may heal
Again with one kind word, tossed down by chance—
And one light kiss can make it bloom with youth.
You can forgive indifference, cold neglect
That left you lone and weary, waiting hours,
Keen wrongs that you did nothing to expect,
And even blows and curses when they leave
No outward marks for all the world to read—
But when he strikes the face he once vowed fair,
Love breaks within the heart, and both do bleed.
Springs bitter Hate, twin-born with burning Shame,
Brings Grief too deep to make the eyelids wet,
As the cold world stares where the kiss once touched
The blushing cheek; and you can ne'er forget,
No, not though sweetest years flow calmly on,
And fair Atonement wanders o'er the scene,
The heart will break with sorrow for days past—
All things are changed from what they once have been.

A WASHERWOMAN.

I do not care! There was a time
    When I put on my Sunday clothes
And went a-walking in the sun,
    Like all these folk who tilt their nose
To see me now. What do I care?
My elbows and my heart are bare!

What does it matter, anyway?
    What does it matter at the end
If you've climbed up and up and up,
    Or have not got one bloomin' friend?
Die with a little prayer of trust
Or with a curse? Both turn to dust.

Why should I be afraid to die?
    I wash and wash the whole year long
The clothes of those who scorn me so,
    And fill my nights with laugh and song.
My hell is day, my heaven is night!
Are not your garments smooth and white?

I wash the sheets from fever's bed;
    The babe's first robes—the flounced skirt
That's whirled in many a glorious waltz,
    And make it clean from the world's dirt.
I charge so little for the score
That though you scorn, you bring me more.

What do I care? My pot of beer
    Is more than all your praise or blame.
My children died, one after one—
    Did I not wash for you the same?
My tears fell fast into the tub
To " rub-a-dub, rub, rub-a-dub! "

They laid one here; they laid one there;
    With stranger's children they knew not;
And I have bought no flowers for them—
    No names are writ to mark the spot.
But as I rub I think and think;
Then night comes on, and I must drink.

UPHEAVAL.

Hark to the wind swift waking in the dark.
Some happy, cosy homestead he'll unroof
And leave the glowing hearthstone dank and cold.
Some old, old tree that stands for many a soul
The symbol of its childhood, youth and love,
Of friends departed like its leaves that fall,
Before the dawn shall totter to its death.
Oh, listen how the windows groan and sigh;
The yellow lamplight flutters up and down,
And round it floats a moth that madly longs
To drown itself in burning floods of light.
The black, black chimney is one hollow roar.
Oh, do not touch my house, thou hungry wind,
For I am calm and happy by my fire,
With all my loved faces gathered round,
And all my dreams that have not changed for years.
I do not wish to change. Pass by, O wind,
Nor drive me from my shelter; I care not
To build another house, however large,
With newer dreams and fires that burn more bright,
And better friends around. Oh, strike some house,
But pass my little dwelling, god of change.
Ah, see! The walls begin to rock and sway,
The wind is stopping here beside my door.
His mighty hammers beat the masonry.
His strident voice sends terror through my blood.
In vain I plead—he cannot hear me call.
His blows fall on my roof invincibly.
He will not go away. " Change, change! " he cries,
And drives me out into the pathless wilds,
All homeless, friendless, old ideals gone,
And no heart for the new ones. On and on,
And never seems a resting-place in view.
It seems eternities since by the fire
I thought my little house so warm, secure,
And all my friends forever, ever mine.
Then I reproach this cruel god of change:
" When all my walls were shattered into dust,
And all my friends and dreams went out from me,
Or I from them—or maybe, each from each,
Oh, god of change, why struck not thou to dust
A little marble shape of Memory
That points its finger backwards as I go?

To take all those, and spare that torturing hand
Oh, cruel god, what means it? " Thus I cry.
He makes no answer. Silently I take
A pile of stones and lay them one on one,
And build them up into another house,
With pain, with sorrow and with labour dear,
A larger house all unfamiliar,
With wider doors and windows that stretch out
As if to grasp at light and air and sun.
But still my old house haunts me. And I sit
Beside my newer fire without my dreams.
How long? For ages, ages, so I think,
And then—a voice, a footfall, and a face
With eyes that smile in mine and seem to know,
And once again I make a circle strong,
And bit by bit creeps back that feeling sweet
Of warm security. Till I forget
That old, old house I dwelt in long ago,
Or just remember that I dwelt in it
As in some other house in other life.
And then once more the wind comes, strong and wild,
And drives me forth again a wanderer.
Until at last I know that in no house
A human soul that grows can live for aye;
Until I shrink no more to hear that far
And sullen rumble rising in the hills,
Nor tremble back before the swelling floods,
Nor hide my eyes before the lightning's blaze,
Nor cower behind a heap of senseless stones
And think they make my world. Blow, blow, O wind,
And take my house and leave me desolate—
If I may grow. Oh, take my crumbling walls
That keep me from the starshine and the sun,
And all the pathless splendours of the world,
The world whose walls are space, space infinite!
Take thou my friend, my lover, or my tree,
Aye, blow my body into dust itself,
If that too be a wall to pen me in,
But give me over all things, Liberty!
O strong, clean wind, I do not fear thee more,
But rise to greet thee when I hear thy voice;
I welcome all upheaval and all change,
However fraught with sorrow and with pain,
That bring my feet into a wider house.
Oh, hail and hail, thou clean, destructive wind!

THE UNBURIED DEAD.

I cannot weep, I cannot pray,
I do not joy me at the day
That once did bring me such delight—
Nor at the little stars at night.

The tiny leaves now seem to sigh
To watch the dawn creep up the sky;
The birds that sing amongst the dew
I think will break my heart in two.

My footsteps have a hollow sound,
As if they fell on churchyard ground,
And so they do—for as I tread
I walk upon myself—long dead.

This is myself who used to sing
And thrill at coming of the Spring,
And look at life with eager eye,
And now I let the world drift by.

I have no hope, I have no fear,
My eyes are calm without a tear—
I hear my friends laugh merrily
And yet it brings no pang to me.

I hear their feet go forth to dance
As though I suffered no mischance,
Those friends who told me should I die
The gracious sun would leave the sky.

They did not break their word—for though
I lie me here so weak and low,
They do not know that I am dead,
For there's no tombstone at my head.

For still my body walks about,
I laugh, and talk, and eat, and shout,
And watch the clock whose fingers say
That I was buried yesterday.

For yesterday—the clock at noon—
I buckled on my prettiest shoon,
And wound a ribbon blue as June
In my brown hair—and hummed a tune.

Oh, wild and sweet the hawthorn spray,
That seemed a thousand things to say,
And there a bird sang such a note
I feared that he would burst his throat.

O softly, silently, I crept
Along the lanes, and as I stepped
Upon a little space of grass,
I heard my lover's footsteps pass.

I hid behind a hawthorn bough,—
How thick and white! I smell it now,—
As dead folk smell the lilies white
That cover coffins up from sight.

And just as I was going to rush
And cry his name—an awful blush
Crept from my heart and stained my brow
It was my last. I know it now.

I heard my dear Elizabeth,
The truest friend that e'er drew breath,
Laugh in his arms. Then all my blood
Swept upwards in a crimson flood.

And then I heard the linnet sing,
" O Spring! O Spring! O Joy, O Spring! "
And there amongst the hawthorn bloom,
I knew that I was in my tomb.

For if the dead can hear at all
That's how they hear a linnet's call;
And by the blood that bathed my sight
I knew that they had slain me quite.

My mother sews my bridal gown,
And every time she lays it down,
She smiles and sighs, so sad and proud;
And does not know she makes my shroud.

For every time I tried to speak
My voice died silently and weak;
I could not tell her that I died
At noon, in all my youth and pride

Elizabeth, my dearest friend,
I'll greet with love until the end,
And Allan, too, both soon and late,
For I've no strength to storm or hate.

I'll smile at them across the street
On each and every time we meet.
Dead women smile behind their veil,
So calm and proud and still and pale.

And when young Robin comes from sea,
Who used to think so much of me,
I'll marry him—he'll never know
That I was dead long, long ago.

And so they'll never guess I'm dead—
For there's no tombstone at my head,
And my dear friend, Elizabeth
Will never know she caused my death.

THE MASK.

Every soul a mask doth wear;
    I have learnt to know it now;
Woven fine with cunning care,
    Shrouding eyes and mouth and brow.

Sometimes, when it proudest seems
    Cruel, satyr-like and grim,
In the soul lie pitying gleams,
    In the heart is anguish dim.

Sometimes when it kindliest smiles,
    There is cruelty more deep
Than the winding serpent's wiles,
    Than the sea where wrecked ones sleep.

Pain and Sorrow slink behind
    Even from the fondest fond;
Like a hurt hare shrinks the mind
    Dreading pity from beyond.

If the mask one moment slips,
    Ah, what grief the soul must know!
Tear-filled eyes and pain-thrilled lips,
    Curses, prayers and raptures show.

Wearing to the gates of death
    This dear mask—oh, journey far!
Laid aside with life's last breath,
    Then, how beautiful men are.

Then their hidden dreams we see,
    All they struggled for and missed,
All their obscure majesty,
    Gods and ghouls they clutched and kissed.

There, without one word to say
    Speak they true 'gainst time and tide,
Caring not for Yea or Nay,
    Unashamed, with mask aside.

A FAREWELL.

Nay, we have had the best, oh lover mine.
Have you not shared my wonder and my dream,
And all my strong-winged thoughts as bright as stars
That thrilled us with the music of their wings?
Have we not talked together, hand in hand,
And climbed the olive hill against the west
To watch the splendours come and wane and die?
My fear is as my love is. Let us part!
So many dreams will vanish in our life,
As sea-foam falls again into the deeps.
Come, let us keep this little dream of ours
To stand besides us when the twilight comes,
Let us not try it up against the edge
Of sharp reality—lest it should die,
For dying once it never lives again.
Some other man I love with lesser love,
With lesser fear to hurt as I care less,
May gather up the flowers you held the first,
I cannot let you keep them till they fade.
For oh, with you I'd fear the thread of grey,
And pluck it as a serpent from my brow,
And fear to lose the music from my voice,
And fear to have you stand beside my bed
To watch my ugly gasping at the last,
And see the cold grey shadows round my eyes,
My eyes filmed o'er with unromantic death.
Why, love of mine, I fear even to die,
Lest love should turn my brave heart cowardly,
And I should cry to death " I will not die! "
I am too fond of peace, and quietly
Would come and go and leave no stir behind,
No slamming of the doors, no passioned cries
To linger after me; but peace, peace, peace.
And I should fear the rags of poverty,
The struggling in the little, noisome streets,
The weary echo of my slip-shod feet
Through little passages to little rooms—
Our love was never meant for little rooms,
Its dwelling place is 'neath the starry heavens,
On great, wide-watered plains where reds and golds
Burn into regal purples with the night.
Or where the moonless forests top the peaks

That seem to prick the littered silvery stars:
By cataracts unfettered should we roam,
And lakes unfathomed, like minor seas,
Or journey into deserts—where there's space
For such a royal love as this of ours.
Ah, think—the thousand, thousand, thousand hearts
As happy and as daring and as young,
Who went to live with courage fine and high
In small dark houses shutting out the sun
And missed their way, and hated at the last!
My fear is as my love is. That is great.
Oh, let us guard this little dream of ours,
And keep it as we keep a memory
Of music chiming o'er a moonlit sea,
Or scent of violets in a valley dim,
Or song of lark we see not in the blue,
Nor kill it by the caging. Let it fly
Away and yet away through boundless heaven,
Its song heard o'er the chilly tide of death,
A sweetness that has known no bitterness,
A dream uncaptured, singing still for us,
Whilst other dreams have long been caged and dumb.
Is it not worth this pang that we shall feel?
Nay, do not hold my hand and harder make
The bitter struggle. Let me go, I pray.
Well, I am free to go. Come, haste, my feet
Turn, eyes, away from the beloved face,
Nor tremble, lips, as if ye begged a kiss.
What agony! But thus we keep a dream,
All unfulfilled, but broken not by fate.
Good-bye again! May you not hold my hand
One little moment that the pain be less?
One moment, then we'll part and save our dream.
Ah, God! You've kissed me and 'tis all undone,
And we must drift with the uncounted throng,
And risk the tiring and the hatred, too.
Oh, traitor, when my heart was growing strong!
But there—what is a dream the more or less?
Suppose we hate? Well, in the depths of hell
There may be souls who strive each one 'gainst each
And yet would never leave the other lone,
Or be left lonely. Here, then is my hand,

173

For love or hatred, sun or rain, or storm,
For little house or all the wide, wide world,
For honour and dishonour—and the tomb,
And at the last, whatever lurks beyond,
If it be heaven, then heaven—and hell, then, hell.
So that they let us see each other's face,
Smiling or scowling, so that we may see.
Another kiss. Oh, love, how could I think
That we might part to save a little dream?
A little dream against this love of ours!

WEARINESS.

How long the day has seemed to heart and rain,
And weary foot that trudges o'er and o'er
A little space of carpet strewn with crumbs,
And hands that ever ply the same old task!
I love them, God knows, but I get so tired!
Too big or little, which art thou, my heart?
O, just to stand upon a high, green hill
And hear the mournful music of the wind
Roll through the valleys clad in sunset mists,
And hear the melancholy peewit's cry
Warning the wanderer from his reedy nest—
With every little prattler fast asleep,
And my own thoughts alone to speak to me,
And find a place within my tranquil breast.
To drink for one brief hour the western lights,
And feel the cool, wet winds caress my cheek,
And blow against my body—and the earth,
So strong and bold, uphold me, mortal frail;
Then let my eye, grown sick of little rooms,
Rove o'er the endless, boundless worlds of space,
With towering and fantastic lands of cloud,
And feel once more Eternity's loved guest;
And a deep peace flow from the quiet hills
Into my heart, too narrow or too wide
For motherhood that dwells in dwarfing rooms,
Until it wearies of its heavy crown,—
Ah, just for this, what would I give to-night?
The hills that bear the little, teasing winds,
And echo back their faintest laugh or sigh,
Should teach me how the mighty, soaring peaks
Scorn not the swift, light clouds that come and go,
And how the furthest echoes of the hill
Cry back again the foolish, lost lamb's plaint
Until its mother finds it. Then my lambs
On my return should marvel at my look,
Quiet, and calm, and strong as those high peaks
That murmur not against the shrouding mists,
But tower above the storm that girds their loins
And smile beneath a crown of sun-shot light.

EPITAPH ON A WORKING WOMAN.

Nothing can disturb her now,
Peaceful heart and peaceful brow;
Smiling through a filmy veil,
Tired eyes closed, and sweet lips pale.
Tired hands folded on her breast
In a little prayer for rest.
Weary ends that would not meet,
Little cares in house and street,
Vexed and helpless wait outside—
Death has claimed her for his bride.
And his house is small and still,
But more sweet than hidden rill
Is his silence, as you rest,
Tired hands crossed upon your breast.

CINDERELLA.

A Modern Version.

The shadows played across her face,
    The firelight flickered red;
The hearth-stone grew a lonely place
    As dwelling of the dead.

Amongst the ashes warm and white
    A cheery cricket sang;
And little winds tapped low and light,
    Homeless but blithe they rang.

Outside, the golden summer moon
    Sailed through a deep green sky;
She listened to the wind's brave tune,
    And could not put it by.

" Oh, fireside light, I've loved thee well
    For many a long, long year.
Thy redness, is it heaven or hell? "
    She cried, in accents drear.

Then rose she from her humble stool,
    And drew the curtains wide,
And saw the shimmering valleys cool,
    The river's moonlit pride!

She left the brown dish to burn black,
    And with uncovered hair,
She walked into the wide-world track,
    With wondering, lovely stare.

" Oh, cricket, in the meadow grass,
    How joyously you sing! "
" So glad am I to see you pass,"
    Chirped back the cheery thing.

" Oh, stream that ripples o'er the stone,
    How sad you sound, yet sweet! "
" Step in, step in, my pretty one,
    And let me lave your feet."

" Oh, heather, heather, dark as blood
　　　Besides the brooding stone,
Where do you get your purple hood? "
　　　The heather made a moan.

"I get my purple from the heart
　　　That lonely wears away;
The last sad drops which from it start
　　　Make one pale, trembling spray.""

Oh, peewit, peewit, circling round,
　　　How mournful is your cry! "
" It is my soul, that echoing sound,"
　　　The peewit made reply.

"Turn back, turn back, thou foolish maid,"
　　　Her godmother then said,
" Back to thy house-tree's shielding shade,
　　　And bake thy batch of bread."

" I'll not go back to mix my dough
　　　With tear-drops tired and hot;
The dish may into pieces go,
　　　And brownies tend the pot."

" My god-daughter, be wise and turn,
　　　The world has many a thorn;
And cares to freeze, and griefs to burn,
　　　And desert lands forlorn."

" But griefs and cares sit on my shelf,
　　　Tho' all are passing small.
Related unto spending pelf—
　　　I'll harbour those more tall.

" There's loneliness in narrow rooms
　　　As well as on the heights;
And hearth-stones that are only tombs
　　　That stay good spirits' flights."

Come griefs, come cares, with mighty wings>
    And arrows tipped with flame;
To meet them, forth my spirit springs—
    They are not mean with shame.

" Come noble joys and noble cares
    To make me stronger grow—
Those rungs of life's eternal stairs
    Up which the great souls go.

" My song may be a song of grief,
    But it shall be my own,
For in its purport is relief;
    Why sigh in undertone?

" Let those of earth attend the fire
    And in their prisons pine;
I seek the stars, high and yet higher,
    To watch their hearth-fires shine.

"God bless you, little lights afar
    Where I have got no place;
I wage for you a holy war,
    And bear with me your grace.

" I fight for those who gaze through tears
    Into the caverns red,
And see the moments, hours, weeks, years,
    Like withered rose-leaves shed."

I bring to them sun, moon and breeze,
    The clean winds from the moor,
And blossoms from the aloe trees,
    And lay them at their door."

UNKNOWN.

They dubbed her queer, and laughed as she went by,
    And knew that she was different in some way,
But still she held her little nook, serene,
    And wore just what she would, and had her say.
She never flinched at speaking out her thoughts,
    Nor ever hated them for scoff and jest,
But took the name of " odd " as if a crown—
    A royal pride within her humble breast.
No numbers to support her, all alone
    She set her face against accepted creeds
Because she deemed it right, and them too weak
    And old and useless like long-withered reeds.
Her grave is lost beneath the hiding grass;
    Her name is graven not on crumbling stone,
But burns immortal 'midst the pioneers,
    Although she lived, and fought, and died unknown.
The famous fields that call Titanic souls
    Know nothing nobler—one neglected spot
She toiled and suffered in, with none to cheer,
    And never cared that she would be forgot.

THE BASTARD DEAD.

He is dead; and the wise elder folk—
    They who think that a bird in a nest
Should be blessed by the priest with his book-
    Calmly say, old and wise, it is best!
He had just learnt to laugh and to coo,
As the babes of the wed mothers do.

From his coming he ever was small,
    With an old-fashioned look in his eyes,
But he filled all my life with his love,
    And we two were more wise than the wise.
When in whispers they spoke of my fall,
His warm lips from my heart sucked the gall.

I had borne the great world's brunt of scorn,
    All its basilisk glances so cold;
And I warmed back my heart's frozen faith,
    At the sun of his head, kinked with gold.
He was Home, he was Friend, he was Love,
With his croon like a white, happy dove!

But oh, what shall I do with my arms,
    And the big, empty space in my breast?
Yet the wise elder folk creeping round,
    Calmly say, old and wise, it is best!
Oh, my soul loved the dear little thing,
Though my finger could boast not a ring.

So I hate them at last for their words,
    That some strong man will now pity me;
Will forgive for a sin he helped not,
    When they bury it darkly with thee!
He had just learnt to laugh and to coo,
As the babes of the wed mothers do.

DAWN.

We have watched through the long darkness for the coming of the
    dawn,
We have dreamed how the first trembling ray would shine
Down upon the misty hollows, where the evil night-owl hoots,
How the light would glide along by peak and pine;
But the long dark hours seem endless, as the famished children
    weep,
And our hearts with wounded hopes are all an-ache,
Yet we beat away the spectre who is whispering in our ears
That the golden light of morn will never break.

Nay we cannot give our hope up. It was born at midnight drear
And it, crooning, fills our lap through sunless hours,
And soft-babbles of the shrouded meads, tired, waiting to reveal
Song of birds, and sheen of streams, and glow of flowers.
Oh, there's something like a glorious bell that rings within the
    soul,
And the mist can never dull its thrilling tone,
Shouting out that Freedom cometh—cometh surely to mankind,
And will throw her sunny rays from zone to zone.

For the world is growing wiser—the sad tears that flood men's
    sight
Help them to clearer vision day by day;
As we clasp hands through the darkness we feel sure that soon or
    late,
O'er the black hill's crest will ride that welcome ray.
And the sobbing of the children will be turned to laughter sweet,
And Woman will go honoured, noble, wise,
Linking arms with Man, her comrade, as the highway opens wide,
When the tears have washed the shadows from our eyes.

SUMMER IN THE SLUMS.

How hot it is! The houses row on row
Bake in the sun's broad glare, which, blinding, pours
On deserts of interminable streets,
With open doors that gasp to the hot air
And beg in vain for one clean, wandering wind!
All day the waggons creak with labouring groan
Across the gritty roads. Not even a tree
Struggles for life amidst this bare, blind grey;
No flower of joyous sap, no hopeful leaf—
Only the children in the alleys play,
Building a short-lived heaven in hell's hot gulfs.
The glaring sky, the burning dusty roads,
Blister the weary faces, weary feet,
Till parched lips moan and sigh, " Oh, God, 'ow 'ot! "
With oaths that fain would open heaven's gate
And burn its cruel, unrelenting laws.
This is sweet Summer that the poets chant,
Singing of hills asheen with moist, deep blue;
Of brown-legged children—careless laughing elves,
Gathering flowers by glassy brooks that flash
And glide through alpine gorges, deep and green
And dark with pine—soft singing as they go
Of far-away unmelted, gleaming snows,
Whilst faery echo answers them their song.
But for the poor, O God, how hot it is!

THE GOSSIP.

Perched in the window seat,
      I watch the people pass,
And listen to their feet;
      The lover and his lass
I spy behind my blind, and tell my heart their joy.

And if, at times, I tell
      The things I overhear—
And add to them, as well,
      Without a pang of fear—
Why, greater folk than I do characters destroy!

I love the murmurs loud;
      The voices far away
That float from a great crowd
      Betwixt the night and day—
The little mystic sounds that follow with their feet.

I merely like to know!
      I strip their motives bare,
And view them, high or low,
      With curious, asking stare,
The mean or mighty souls that dwell within one street.

I watch the people walk,
      In sun, in rain, in sleet;
And then of them I talk,
      Now bitterly, now sweet,
So do the men who write great books that the world reads.

The lover who betrays,
      He fears me in his heart;
I read its hidden ways;
      The whispering I first start—
And on its rustling track the wedding day he speeds.

And as the hearse creeps past
      I read the Dead's sealed book,
From first page to the last,
      And bid the watchers look!
So do biographers of those who've served us well!

Music is talk in notes,
            Pictures in colours fair,
Though they be finer thoughts,
            And sweeten more the air,
They are but talk, at most, and silence wields her spell.

Why should I hold my tongue?
            I help full many a cause,
And hinder many a wrong,
            As well as written laws!
The time will come when all lie dumb beneath a stone!

If I some wrong have done,
            Some good I've also worked;
I've watched, in shade or sun,
            Nor e'er that duty shirked.
More room, and I, maybe, had been a mighty one!

I might have struck down lies
            With patience and with strength,
Till they no more might rise—
            And shown the truth, at length —
Tattle might be a god in wider chambers bred.

What cared I for my home?
            But others I loved well!
For them I far would roam,
            Some wondrous thing to tell;
I might have reared (who knows!) in Parliament my head.

To talk and not to do
            Is genius in its way,
In sun, or rain, or blue,
            To loiter day by day,
And get half-way to nowhere—and then turn back again.

So had I been a man
            I should have passed, I know,
(I do the best I can!)
            To where, all in a row,
The speakers, not the doers, pour forth the thundering strain!

CRADLE SONG.

Grow strong, grow strong, my darling child,
    O how I love thee, infant small!
Yet my heart throbs more warm and wild
    To think thou growest strong and tall.

I'll tell thee of the singing pine
    That's black against the sunset red,
And where the little fairies dine,
    And how the fire-fly lights their bed.

I'll tell thee of the sun and rain;
    How rainbows spread across the sky;
How Winter decorates the pane;
    And of the frog with beauteous eye.

The summer grass is green and long;
    The summer sky is bright and blue;
The summer birds sing many a song,
    And we will sing together, too.

Grow strong, grow strong, my baby sweet!
    I'll guard thee as an infant small,
But yearning comes with constant beat
    To see thee grow more strong and tall.

A secret tear may leave mine eye
    To see thee leave me more and more,
And pass at last, without a sigh,
    To the wide world without the door.

But grow thou strong, oh, branch of me,
    Till from my tender timbers young
An arrow for pure liberty,
    Divinely made, at greed is flung.

Better thy death for honour's sake,
    The lowering cloud of worldly scorn,
The flesh to waste, the heart to break,
    Than leave the world as if unborn.

Grow strong and tall for noble grief,
    The world has need, my son, of men,
Though sometimes, trembling like a leaf,
    I may wish thee a child again.

THE CHILDREN OF THE POOR.

Have you ne'er seen some sweet-breathed flow'r
    That trembled high o'er world of grey?
Nor felt the next bleak wind would shower,
    And blow its beauty bright away?
Such is the brief and fragile joy
    Of poor folk's children—blossoms fair!
Chill winds of Care and Toil destroy
    The innocence that comes—from where?

Have you ne'er seen the dewy crown
    That decks the branches of the thorn,
And feared to see it sliding down
    To leave their blackness all forlorn?
E'en as we gaze the bough is shook
    By ruthless breeze or careless wight—
The thorn is naked when we look,
    And vanished its translucent light!

But oh, how sad it is to know
    That childhood, coming not again,
Should lose its happy youthful glow,
    All for an idle dream of gain;
That sunny worlds of magic green
    Where fairies laugh and dance and play
Should turn into a smoke-grimmed scene,
    Where Joy and Beauty fly away.

The children of a newer day
    Whose light e'er now comes o'er the brink
Of this dark night, with faint, pure ray,
    Shall deep of dreaming glories drink.
The sheath shall guard the tender soul
    Till strong, mature—then, flung aside,
The slow-won colours of the whole
    Shall be the nation's joy and pride.

OLD WOMAN'S SONG.

This is the meaning of growing old—
    Faltering feet that used to fly;
Blood that chills with the winter cold;
    Threading your needle with aching eye;
Tired as a lone ship adrift on the sea!
Weary, so weary! Ah, me!

This is the meaning of growing grey—
    Losing your children one by one;
Wedded, and buried, or living away;
    Like an old tree, when its leaves are gone.
None to say " Rest you," how tired you be,
Weary, so weary! Ah, me!

FAITHS OUTWORN.

There is no sadder hour in all our lives
    Than when we find the spirit has outgrown
Some creed, or faith, which in the by-gone days
    Has seemed sufficient for its joy alone.
And every soul has got its lumber-room
    Where worn-out garbs of thought are laid aside
When by some burst of sunlight pure and strong
    It finds they are not meet for cleanly pride.
The gentle and the weak bring lavender
    With which awhile to keep the moths away,
Stroke their worn folds with tender hands and sigh,
    " They were the world to us but yesterday! "
But they perchance more noble and more strong
    Cry " Take them, Time, for they are thin and old;
We have outgrown them and we need them not,
    For they no longer shield us from the cold.
Take them into thy ragbags of the past,
    For every precious thing we've picked away
To make more beautiful a garment new—
    Take them, O Time, for they have had their day."

THE GIFT.

There is one who will ask but of you that you bring her back beads
    from the sea;
There is one who will ask but of you that you sing her gay songs in
    the dusk;
There is one who will ask but of you that you walk tall and proud
    at her side,
By the door of her rival who laughs, where her old lover sits in the
    porch;
There is one who will ask but of you that you love her by night and
    by day,
Who is weary, and waiting, and lone—and would e'en make the
    best of the worst!
There is one who will ask for your soul, but like quicksilver keep
    back her own.
But for me, I ask nothing at all,—save the sound of your voice in
    the gloom,
As you pass by my door to their doors, with a curse at your horse
    as he slips,
'Neath your hurried impatience to fly by my dark, insignificant
    door.
For the love that is love overmuch may win nothing—just nothing
    at all,
But the curse in the heart of the night and the longing to get by
    the door.

A FIRESIDE FANCY.

Let my house be one of a little row
Where I hear the people pass to and fro
    Behind thin walls of plaster—
Hear them laugh, and sing, and rake up the fire
When the air is chill, and the wind mounts higher;
    And almost their hearts beat faster.

Let me hear the tramp of their children's feet,
The innocent laughter so shrill and sweet,
    And the old brown cradle swinging;
Let me muffle my tread and hush my breath
As over their threshold steps life and death,
    The sound or the silence bringing.

For there waits my house in a little row
Where I shall hear no one pass to and fro,
    Nor sound of laughter or weeping—
'Twixt walls that echo no neighbour's knock,
That never can thrill to the cradle's rock,
    Between neighbour and neighbour sleeping.

A MODERN MAGDALEN.

'Twas God made me so beautiful, and man shut me away,
Like a red rose in a small, dark room to wither day by day,
And the devil put into my heart the hot little whisper " Nay."

The others sang, and joked, and talked until the day was done,
But I sighed as I watched the free birds fly or a passing shaft of
    sun,
And the spotted mirror upon the wall made strange thoughts
    through me run.

For the face I saw in the misty glass had a halo round its head,
Its eyes were still lakes, sapphire-blue; its mouth, carnation red;
And it did not look like the face of a girl to have nothing but daily
    bread.

When I passed the rich man's garden as to work I slowly came,
I spied through hedges, dimly green, a many-coloured flame;
And knew that the tulip's sun-loving heart and my own heart were
    the same.

The God who made the violet that loves the moist, cool shade,
He made the heart of the tulip that is gold-splashed and unafraid,
So the tulip is planted to catch the sun as a thing for the sunshine
    made.

Grey were the walls of the workroom, where, in the summer's heat,
The tired flies crawled so wearily to the drone of the noisy street,
And I heard, to the whizz of the whirling wheel, my own heart's
    weary beat.

And a weary fear did clutch me of growing grey and bent
As the woman who worked next to me with a dreary, sad content,
And who never knew when the sky was blue, and whose life was a
    lengthened Lent.

So I wandered away and left it, and found it easy to go,
With the light of the beauty God gave me, and the scorn and the
    whispers low,
And the door of the friend that was shut in my face, and the
    flattery of my foe.

O God, I am very sinful, and I've nothing at all to say,
Save " The floor of the workroom was dusty, the walls of the
    workroom grey,
And men for the sake of their bankbooks were grinding my beauty
    away.

" The gift of a wonderful beauty should be for the meek, or the
    free,
Or the prisoners who pine in the prisons may sell it in misery;
With God's beauty, hard toil, and the devil—oh,where was the
    chance for me? "

I loved all the mystic beauty that shines in a thousand things,
The flower that grows by the roadway—the rainbow glitter of rings,
And the cool, stately beauty of marble, and the glory of butterflies'
    wings.

It was only a chance. I took it. The light was a fading fire,
And not the big sun I had wanted. It flickered and died in the
    mire.
And it may be my fall was the greater for heights I had dared to
    aspire.

It may be the pride in my bosom, and the hatred of it all,
(Whilst good folk drudging and praying were thankful for things so
    small)
Is the force that shall lift the dead level more near to its ultimate
    goal?

That shall sound like a trumpet pealing o'er Patience, fear and
    cant,
And make them ready to risk things, to snatch at the sun they
    want—
I failed, and went down in the darkness. I fell, and I know they
    shan't.

DIANA'S SONG.

O swift, mad joy of the flying wood
    And cataract's thundering roar!
And the glassy green where the April flood
    Stands still by a sedgy shore.
But mine is the rushing and rapturous joy
That the cataract knows, or the heart of a boy.

The brushwood crackles as I tear by
    And the birds fly from their nest,
And the violets breathe forth a scented sigh
    As I disturb their rest,
But mine is the joy of the travelling wind
That is daring and bold, that you never can bind.

O laughing Cupid, I have no fear;
    Go shoot your timorous maids,
Born not for the blush, the sigh, or the tear,
    I am queen of the woodland glades!
For mine is the joy of the glorious sea
That is tossing forever, immortal and free.

No burning passion shall hunt me down
    To ceaseless, restless care,
Nor my heart bleed deep at a master's frown—
    I am free as the virgin air.
And who then would barter such freedom as this
For the frail, fleeting joy that is found in a kiss?

O swift, mad joy of the flying wood,
    And cataract's thundering roar!
And the glassy green where the April flood
    Stands still by a sedgy shore.
But mine is the rushing and rapturous joy
That the cataract knows, or the heart of a boy.

EIGHTEEN.

Shimmering land of beauty and romance
    Locked with a fairy key,
Over whose flower-strewn sward what light feet dance—
    But mine no more, ah, me!

What scented winds sway gaily blossomed trees
    Almost within the reach,
Then swing them upwards in a laughing breeze—
    Bright blossoms like the peach!

Unearthly shells are scattered by its shore
    That sing into the ear
Sweet songs that I shall hear, O, nevermore!
    Sweet songs that have no fear.

There, star-white feet through sunny waters walk,
    And glad hands garlands weave,
Whilst silvery voices chime in merry talk
    That leaves no time to grieve.

How quickly dry the tears of rainbow sheen!
    For Hope her home makes here,
In this fair country that we call Eighteen—
    She strings each glittering tear.

What boat was that which bore us far away
    From this sweet shrine of dreams,
With only memory, one pure, scented spray
    Snatched from its sunlit streams?

What boat is that shall bear us back again?
    Back to its first, fresh green,
And blossoms never beaten by the rain?
    Seas soundless flow between.

PAST.

I have been loved, I would not die,
    Or call to Death because Love went,
Bidding him seal my weary eye.
    Love, passing, kissed me. Rest content,

Thou mateless heart within my breast
    That sees the brushwood bursting green,
And sighs above an empty nest!
    Some would be glad that love had been.

Let the loud rains beat long and drear,
    And hoarse winds shout from scar to scar,
Love has gone by—I need not fear
    Again to lose him at the bar.

Love has gone by. I shall not miss
    Him in the labyrinths of the wood;
Warm on my lips he left his kiss,
    And still it burns there, red as blood.

I made for him no golden chains;
    I did not even whisper " Stay!"
I watched him fly o'er distant plains,
    And knew that I had had my day.

Let rolling seas strive to the sky,
    No hopes of mine are there to sink!
I stand no more with aching eye
    To watch the ships come o'er the brink.

I have been loved. I do not weep
    That love went by upon the wind.
An hour of love is high and deep,
    And who the rose's scent may bind?

I do not dread the bed of dust;
    I do not fear the chilly dark—
Love's kiss was warm with hope and trust,
    And joyous as the soaring lark.

A DREAM GARDEN.

Had I a garden it should be a-blow
    With poppies scarlet red,
Have hedges high, a place where I might go
    When all seemed dull and dead;
A blaze of colouring gorgeous as the glow
    Of sunsets overhead.

There should be sunflowers tall with crowns of gold,
    And spikes of lilies rare;
The mosses green from hill, and field, and wold
    Should richly nestle there;
There should be silvery margu'rites, quaint and old,
    And roses blightless fair.

Love-in-a-Mist should droop its heads of blue
    O'er ladlove smelling sweet;
Carnations plenty bloom there, dashed with dew,
    And the rich " Tweet! tweet! tweet! "
Come from a nestling bird, with the faint sough
    Of all sweet airs and fleet.

Flowers for all moods; the lilies purely white
    For when the soul turned saint;
Roses to fill the heart with glad delight
    For love that knows no taint;
To droop with, soar with, red and blue and white—
    And love without restraint.

A LITTLE GIRL.

Let me try," she eager said,
      Voice a-tremble with desire
Sweet as fairy fingers swept
      O'er a silver, hidden lyre,
Upward look of hope and fear;
Half a smile, and half a tear!
" I'll be gone five by-and-by.
I can do it. Let me try! "

" Let me try! " Ah, little girl,
      With the eyes of harebell blue,
And an elf in every curl,
      Much to try awaiteth you.
Life and Love and Death, I see,
Beauteous, awful Trinity;
Do not fear you will be late.
Wait a moment, darling, wait!

You shall have your hair up, sweet,
      Fastened with a jewelled comb;
Wear a gown down to your feet;
      Further than the garden roam!
Keep your fairies whilst you may,
In the golden land of play;
When that time comes by-and-by,
You will laugh, but we shall sigh.

Noble joys and cares shall sit
      In your heart—grown wide with years;
Saddest tears be rainbow lit;
      Brightest smiles be tinged with tears.
Land where mother can redress you,
With magic kisses heal and bless you,
Is the land, the pilgrims say,
(Pilgrims old and bent and gray)
Where divide tears, smiles, you may—
Where the happy fairies play.

THE BUILDING.

"Nay, strike not back—Forbear," my mother said,
    " 'Tis woman's part to suffer and forgive;
To kiss the striker fierce and passionate,
    That gentler, sweeter thoughts in him may live."
She was a woman cast in mildest form,
    Who would have loved the dog that bit her hand,
And ever strove to quell the healthful storm,
    And bring with words of love the boat to land.
I did not wish to wound her, so I turned
    And kissed my brother with a Judas kiss,
Whilst in my heart the fires of anger burned,
    One righteous, honest, noble blow to miss!
I learned to smile, to run away and fear
    My comrade, who could never understand
Why his injustice brought the weakling tear;
    Why I withheld, controlled, my upraised hand.
I grew, and grew, and learned to smile so well,
    They thought within my pretty careless head
No thought there was—my heart, as fierce as hell
    In its rebellion, innocent—and dead!
I fought my foes with smiles and dulcet words
    That held a hidden poison—turned my neck
So that my jewels trembled; sang like birds
    In summer woods—man's happiness to wreck.
I never asked for justice then, but stole
    A mean revenge—made helpless with a kiss
This Titan, who had been a brother soul,
    Betrayed him, scorned him, slew him—grew to this,
This shimmering serpent form, of haunting guile,
    Because I stayed the blow, and learned to smile.

CIVILIZATION.

A bust of Clytie in a windowed niche;
    A chat of some new flower cult, or the stars;
A babel of the nation's mingled tongues;
    From splendid, frowning Beethoven some bars
Sounding like waves upon a rocky shore—
" How grand is Life," cry two, or three, or four.

Out in the street, hoarse-voiced the flower girl cries
    Poet's narcissus, with a shuddering breath,
Clutching with claw-like hands her sieve-worn shawl
    And on her face the pallid look of death,
Or else the purple flush that comes from gin;
Some sculptor carve her, then! Nay, she's too thin.

Look at the faces by the city lamp—
    Pride, greed, servile humility and whine;
The lean professor yellow as his books,
    The navvy dull—the joyful one, from wine!
The idler bored to death, the stitcher pale,
The unloved child whose language is a wail.

Is this then our grand climax? Was our toil
    Up through the countless ages but for this?
That some may wear the flower, but most the thorn?
    Then Progress lured us with a wanton's kiss!
What, all these struggles, failures, lessons taught
For one fine scholar—and the others, naught?

All this, the gem-like rooms of colour rare,
    The magic beauty of the poet's word,
May come to one—whilst endless hovels stretch
    Through streets where music's voice is never heard?
This weary march up dizzy steeps of time
For one flower's subtle scent—and all this slime?

Had we not better stayed beside our fire
    In the dim cave, low down beside the beast,
And shared his calm content, his savage power,
    Wandered beside the lake, and to the east,
That streamed with unknown fires as day begun,
Out-stretched our lithe, strong arms to greet the sun?

Sun-worship! Now, men worship barren gold,
　　Tread bloody, worldly ways o'er human hearts,
To count their wealth by figures in a book,
　　And praise a nation for its clustered marts,
Great God, keep me a pagan; in this night
Of Mammon-worship, let me worship light.

But no, Nature or God would never mock
　　The creatures, born with pain, to die with pain,
And force them through these endless grooves of change
　　Without some noble end, some glorious gain;
Some hope to reach the lowest, weakest, worst,
The trampled, branded, loathed, self-hated, curst!

These jewelled, perfumed robes and beggar's rags
　　Will pass away, and fettered Art steal forth
From private prisons out into the streets
　　That all may see her beauty and her worth.
The gatherer of the orchard will sing clear
The mighty master's music, with tuned ear.

And she who sells narcissus in the rain
　　Will set them in blue bowls in Springtime room,
And love the faint, far scent that now she hates,
　　And walk the native vales where first they bloom
And for the first time in this vaunted land
Labour and Love and Art walk hand in hand.

THE HERETIC.

I am a Heretic, they say. They drag me through the summer day
Towards my burning. Is it true? O Jesu, but the sky is blue!
Death is so cold, and Life so warm. How could I do them any
    harm?
A simple soul who just spake out a simple thought, nor dreamed
    of Doubt,
What was it that they feared? One word—one little word, then
    naked sword,
The knotted rope around my wrist which yesterday my lover
    kissed,
And every eye shows fear and scorn which smiled and worshipped
    yestermorn.
Only my dog—the dog that he was jealous of— keeps close by
    me—
Jesu! They've stabbed him! There—he tears the man who stabbed.
    Ha! ha! my prayers!
I know not that my heart could feel such bitter hate, cold, fierce as
    steel.
Thy pardon, Mary, mother mild—they've killed my dog, mine from
    a child!
O, frightened heart, how fast you beat to hear the tramping of
    their feet,
Thronging from high place and from low, to see me tortured as I
    go!
What was it that I sudden spoke? T'was to my lover, and my yoke
Was just his arms, and swift I said—What was it, brain? He
    turned his head
And gave me one long, awful look, as on a leper, then he took
His crucifix from out his breast, and left me. This is all the rest,
This surging crowd. And how they hiss! Who told them, then?
    There was his kiss
Hovering above me, and I said, as to a soul my soul had wed,
A simple word or two that came into my mind like radiant flame.
I know it lit me through and through, and then he groaned—O
    sky, how blue!
And worst of all, I cannot think what 'tis I die for, on the brink
Of this dark death. What was't I said? This blessing, Lord! He
    turned his head—
Ah, me, 'tis gone, and to the pyre I go, nor know why bums the
    fire.
Will someone know who sees it leap, and catch it as it haunts
    their sleep?

But as for me, I have forgot. I only fear, and feel the knot,
And hear their hungry, hungry cries ring upwards to the smiling
skies.
And yesterday they spoke me fair. Oh!—There an idiot pulled my
hair,
A foolish idiot, whom I tossed a silver coin once. All is lost.
He pulled the hair my lover loved—and he stood by and never
moved,
And watched the idiot's leering grin. And I—I watched him, and
his chin
Was trembling. Should men tremble so, and lift no finger when we
go,
When mud is thrown, and then a stone? Stand still with but a
foolish groan,
Whilst my dog followed? As he stood and saw my brow daubed
with my blood,
The brow he called a pearl—pure moon, and kissed, and kissed,
and ne'er had done,
He shuddered like a frightened child, with pallid lips and eyes all
wild.
I pitied him. Quick! Let me die before my Love itself goes by!
Quick! Let me feel the burning flame whilst there is sweetness in
his name.
Ah, me, 'tis gone, dear Lord, 'tis gone, with empty heart I die
alone—
For something that I have forgot, ah, me, upon the very spot
Where at the fountain's misty fall I laughed and sang to toss my
ball.
The fire! My hair, it takes my hair! O Grief, O Pain, O mad Despair!
My brain—it reels—I hear my screams like horrid echoes heard in
dreams.
My brain! My brain is bursting! Why—*I now remember why I die.*
It comes again, the living thought. Oh, Joy, I do not die for nought!

THE GREAT MAN'S WIFE.

Always the crowd, the crowd, from first to last;
    The crowd that crowns and scourges in an hour,
And rends and fawns, with great chameleon mind
    That changes colour with the ruling power;
The crowd he loved and toiled for, thrusting e'en
    The god-like love to take a second place
Before his thought for them—pressing from streets
    Of hutch-like houses to behold his face.
Their ceaseless knock was ever on our door,
    Their ceaseless inroads through his heart, with Care
Preceding them, yet fondest Love before
    With torch-light clear—though oft behind . Despair!
And half the little love he gave to me
    Was thrown in moments as I sat and heard
With gentle patience all his plans for them,
    The outside throng. How all his spirit stirred
At thought of them, the People! Yet had he
    One syllable let fall too great, obscure,
Lo! how their clapping would have changed to stones,
    And all forgotten been grand work and pure.
What was their love to mine? A puff of smoke
    Changed by the movement of the fickle wind
And scattered into air, but mine was rock
    Deep-rooted in the earth, and firm reclined.
He had not space for e'en a country rest,
    Or where the sea's white breakers rushing proud
Eternally are craving. He felt lone
    As in a desert, absent from the crowd.
He said a crowd was just a single soul
    With many moods, he knew, yet one clear soul
As the vast sea that smiles or surges wild
    Is one great salt tide from the furthest pole.
He loved them so! Right to the very end
    His heart was with them. As I leaned to catch
The last faint echo of his fading voice
    And heard the restless ticking of his watch
Beneath the pillow, suddenly he said
    " They come at eight," and with the words fell dead;
Without one word to me, one little word
    To bear through years as barren as before!
And then I heard the voices of the crowd
    Who came to ask his welfare at the door.

Not even grief is mine alone. They come
    And plead to share my tears, this mighty crowd,
In which not one doth wish as I do now
    To follow where he leads in cold, wan shroud.
His voice has sunk to silence—in a while,
    A very little while, they will forget,
And he will be all mine, and memory
    Will live in just one heart—her eyes still wet.

LOST DREAMS.

Where do they flee to, those sweet dreams departed
    We loose on the air like a brood of bright doves,
With their eyes full of mystery and dew-gleam and fire-flame,
    God-like aspirations—fair, unfulfilled loves?
The songs that elude us, too sweet for the singing,
    That flit by and will not be netted in words?
There's surely some valley of green, slumb'rous shadow
    Where angels of hope tend our broken-winged birds!

Somewhere and sometime the tired world shall find them,
    Shall catch the glad beat of their home-coming wings!
All the songs that were sung not, the loves that were crowned not,
    As if through the silence some god touched the strings.
From out that dim valley where sound murmuring waters,
    Where burns not the sunshine, where drips not the rain,
The dreams that we lost on a far-away morning
    Shall come pure and whole to the world once again.

Dante, who gazed hollow-eyed after Beatrice;
    Beethoven, the king whom a woman disdained—
They who gave to the world all the song of their passion,
    In winning had lost; in the losing had gained!
Great hearts that are broken by sorrows, thick falling,
    Crushed low by the heels of the leaden despairs,
Have flung in their suffering sweet odours immortal,
    As angels might swing high on heaven's shining stairs!

Fair dreams that were bred of our love and our longing,
    It is not in vain that we pay the great cost;
For to-day or to-morrow some sad one will find them—
    Since someone will find them they cannot be lost.
In yonder green valley deep down 'twixt the mountains
    Their wings will grow strong for the journey to be;
When floats the low whisper of "Now the world needs you! "
    Our dreams will come forth for the whole world to see.

HOME THIRST.

With Apologies to Gerald Gould.

The white road wanders up and down beneath the sun and moon,
And sure the one would follow it were crazy as a loon;
For if we danced our lives away; or at the least, our shoes,
We found not half so much, I trow, as what the heart must lose.

West for the one who's of the West, South for the one who's South;
But Northern names taste sweet to me as honey in the mouth;
One sprig of heather from our moors for all your pine-topped hills,
And for your cataract's thundering might—one gem-drop from our
    rills!

I know not where the white road runs, and just as little care,
Except that it creeps loving back, to home, and all that's there;
Yes, dear are all the winding ways, wherever they may roam,
For North, or South, or East or West, they every one lead Home.

KNOWLEDGE.

I am not sorry to have quaffed the cup
    Filled with the honey and aloes of life;
Dear as I loved the country of cool shade,
    Not to have missed the city's heat and strife.
Glad to have wandered, poor amongst the poor,
    And in the anguish of my sisters' moan
Stretched helping hands, forgetful of my need,
    And known their sorrow greater than my own.

Glad to have felt the sting of unearned blame
    If that has taught my lips to be more kind;
Nor ever wish that life had kinder been
    If I grew strong with fighting 'gainst the wind.
Glad to have known the homesick loneliness,
    And wandered through the night that had no star,—
Better to plunge into the unknown sea
    And learn the worst—than loiter at the bar.

O cup of pain, and tears, and knowledge dear,
    That flowed like fire along each throbbing vein;
Galvanic heat that thrilled me through and through
    I would not have my innocence again.
Glad to have quaffed where million lips have been,
    I, laughing, lift the goblet in my hand,
Whilst all my spirit casts a bright, brave smile,
    That it has drunk—and learned to understand!

ETERNITY.

I sought this angel, whose deep eyes
    Are sparks of everlasting fire—
Pursuing through star-littered skies
    Until my mortal feet did tire.

Then in the tales of mighty men
    With courage flaming as the sun,
Whose iron heel tramped the ferny glen—
    Death stamped them low as day was done!

I sought him still, in cloisters grey,
    With moss-grown tablets half-erased,
That echoed now to childish play,
    Yet ever fled the form I chased.

The hours seemed only as the leaves
    That, trembling, decked the tree of Time;
E'en as the whispering aspen grieves,
    Then drops into the slow stream's slime.

Until two hands beneath my chin
    Raised up my saddened face to his,
The priceless crown of love to win—
    Eternity within a kiss!

The castle crumbles, dour and grey,
    A wreck within a waveless sea;
That kiss shall bear me up alway
    Through cycles of Eternity.

O'er golden roads of suns untold,
    My mortal feet unharmed will pass
Amongst the blazing stars of old,
    As if but daisies in the grass.

Oh, angel of the haunting eyes,
    Thou pourest out thy mystic bliss,
Freely for all below the skies,
    Immortals are we—by a kiss.

The sallow, scrubbing servant girl
    Becomes a holy, lovely thing
Wherein the soul doth bright unfurl
    To hear the rushing of Love's wing.

The dusty workman, bent and pale,
    Who sighs to hear the whistle's shriek,
Sails in a ship of purple sail
    As his tired wife doth kiss his cheek.

And children's kisses! Could we see
    These unseen angels as they go,
How sweet and shining would they be,
    All robed in innocence, like snow.

And mother's kisses! Did we sink
    Into hell's farthest, darkest spot,
Her tears would be our fieriest drink,
    Her kiss would bless and burn us not.

A life is not a little flower
    With which a blind child's hand doth play
Pulling the petals, hour by hour,
    And laughing as they blow away.

The clock that ticks upon the wall,
    The calendar of months and years,
Are crumbling to a mighty fall;
    They mark not off our sighs and tears.

Whole centuries of deepest joy
    Meet in one tiny moment's space,
As some but lately dreaming boy
    Sees by the sun his sweetheart's face.

We need not go to Juliet's tomb,
    Or hers within that city gay,
Who buried low her youthful bloom,
    Watering with tears both night and day.

Yon faltering pair who cross the street,
    Whose pulse now beateth faint and slow,
Breathe odours that are passing sweet,
    Like roses buried under snow.

Not books, nor war's steel-knitted breast,
    Nor gold though piled deep as the sea,
But just a kiss, when life is best,
    Shall save our souls immortally.

THE COQUETTE.

I win men's hearts with a little sigh,
With the quivering lash of a downcast eye,
Then I toss them away with a mocking laugh,
Oh, as if they were only so much chaff!
And what is their pain is my dancing joy,
And the boy of an hour back is no more a boy.

I was born in the world with a mighty thirst,
And within my soul is a room accurst,
Where love never steps with his dimpled feet,
With his gleaming arrows and laughter sweet,
And over the door of that room is writ
" Conquest " and with flame every letter is lit.

Yet I envy the lovers who saunter by
When the bright stars burn in the deep, green sky,
Who can see only one in a world so wide,
Whilst my heart is that of the shifting tide,
That is never true to one narrow shore,
But wins them, and scorns them for evermore.

When I was a child beside the brook
The pebbles up from their bed I took,
And I wondered why all their colours had fled,
Then I cast them back on the brook's chill bed,
But my sister kept hers for many a day,
And wept when she lost it in childish play.

I think the sirens who sit and sing
By river and ocean in fitful spring
And draw with their music the brave ships down
Whilst the women wait in the distant town,
Must sometimes grieve in the midst of their glee
For wrecks that they sink in the sunless sea;

Must sometimes ask why so selfishly,
Forever attract, forever deny,
Why I here wait alone on the iron rock
Just to draw the ships to the dreadful shock,
Whilst faithful women who wait in the town
Are forgotten for me, and the ships go down.

I think that sometimes, or soon or late,
The men I have drowned with the kiss of fate
Will send me a soul that shall laugh at my cry,
That will heed not my moaning, but let me die;
And the wraith of the siren left unkissed
Shall vanish away in the peaceful mist.

WHILST ONE REMAINS.

Whilst there is left in this broad land of ours
One hungering child, be it for bread or flowers,
Though all the rest go happy 'neath the skies,
A stain across our country's honour lies
    Whilst one remains.

Within a world of women pure and sweet
Whilst there's one wretched outcast on the street
Selling the fragments of her soul for bread,
The rest by lower paths must aye be led,
    Whilst one remains.

Though we have access to the finest thought
One darkened mind, unlettered and untaught,
Throws its dull shade across our stolen light.
Turns half our sunny pleasure into night,
    Whilst one remains.

Though all life's sweetest joys were poured on me
I could not 'scape the brand of slavery;
My quivering soul must wear the festering chains
Must feel the slave's hot tears and bear his pains,
    Whilst one remains.

WAITING.

Oh, I think of a myriad things
    As I wait for his coming at night,
With the child in its cradle asleep,
    Like a rose-bud—so lovely and white;
With an agonised cry round the house
    From the restless, dissatisfied wind,
Till I think it is maybe her ghost
    On a visit, some comfort to find.

For once she sat as I sit here now,
    With a hope and a fear deep within,
With a start at the red cinder's fall,
    And a clasp of her hands, pale and thin;
Then she hearkened the wind round the house,
    And the clock with its slow, steady boom,
Till she shivered and wondered the while
    If there was but herself in the room.

In her life-time we two never met;
    There is only a picture hangs there
Of her face that was anxious and worn
    'Neath the crown of her heavy, dark hair;
But I sometimes feel that she is near,
    And waits here for him also with me;
That she knows all the grief in my heart,
    And is sorry as woman can be.

Well, she bore him no infant, at least,
    To lie hushed on her bosom, and smile,
Till her eyelids drooped heavy with tears,
    At the thought of the world and its guile.
Oh, the sorrow if it should grow foul,
    And its innocence suffer the stain!
She may sleep in her grave without fear,
    Whilst my heart has its love and its pain.

Oh, so weary for slumber am I!
    I alone such a vigil must keep;
Nay, my soul, there are many as sad,
    And like me, they must listen and weep;
And a terror as piercing as fire
    Grips the heart as the door is flung wide,
And a purple-faced tyrant sprawls in
    With a growl like a maniac's pride.

So I think of a myriad things,
    Of his old mother gentle and frail,
She who thinks of him still as a child
    That she rocked at her breast, soft and pale.
Then I think of the falsehoods I tell
    In the letter I send her each week,
That he's steady and good as can be—
    With the mark of his hand on my cheek!

And I think of the bright, bonnie days
    When I lived with my sweet sisters three,
And we sang like four larks in the spring,
    Surely none were so happy as we!
Of the roses we pinned at our waists,
    The gay ribbons we twined in our hair,
And the lilt of the merry, old tunes
    In the days all unshadowed by Care.

My dear Mary! she died in her youth,
    And kind Nell who came next, lives away,
And she bears a new baby each year,
    Whilst sweet Susan is lonely and gray,
As she stitches and stitches for bread,
    And the people who lodge her are queer,
She has lost the free laughter and jest
    And has taken to saving, I hear.

Yes, this life is a weird tangled skein
    As I sit here and ponder at night;
There are threads that are red as heart's blood
    There are threads that are black—but few bright.
'Tis a puzzling and troublesome task
    To make out just the course they all run,
And I give up at last, with the hope
That it's somehow all right when life's done.

My dear Mary! she died in her youth,
    Ere the gold had gone out of her hair,
Whilst the laughter came light to her lips
    And her heart was unwithered by care.
It is we who live on change the most,
    For we die every day that we live,
But we grow in the process, I trust,
    And one lesson we learn—to forgive.

Hush! for that was his step in the street!
    And he soon now will fling back the door;
Will he come like a whirlwind in March,
    Or just fall like a log to the floor?
Well, the morning will come round at last,
    And the house will be quiet and grey;
Oh! I'm thankful to think in my heart
    That his mother won't know far away.

A LULLABY.

Without Apologies to Sir Walter Scott

O hush thee, my baby, thy sire was a slave,
Whom overwork thrust in the dark, early grave;
The gloomy, grey streets from this den which we see,
Are hungrily waiting, dear baby, for thee.
O hush thee, my baby.

O sleep whilst thou may, babe, by night and by day,
Thy pale mother rests not, but stitches away;
There's no one to guard thee from hunger but she,
Her tears flowing silently all for thee.
O hush thee, my baby.

O hush thee, my baby, through days dark and wild
Stream sun-shafts of glory that can't be defiled;
The marching of myriads is borne to our ears,
And we will march with them, and sing through our tears.
O hush thee, my baby!

FOR THOSE IN PERIL ON THE SEA.

O bring them back from wind and wave,
    To wife and mother, babe, and friend,
Where sweet home faces bend above,
    There let our dear ones find their end!
The waves roll up from mighty gulfs,
    But here we kneel and pray to Thee,
Whilst loud winds whistle through the aisles,
    For those in peril on the sea.

The coppery sky lowers closely down;
    The thunders roll, the lightnings flash;
Deep shades or lurid glare we see,
    And hear with pain the billows dash.
O bring them home, where land-sounds break,
    To toil once more, our stay to be,
Where we may tend them let them pass,
    And save them from the raging sea!

Back to the flickering, cheerful fire,
    The babe's warm fingers clinging tight;
The wifely welcome at the door,
    As from their toils they trudge at night.
Sweeter than scents of soil and flowers
    Our loved ones' lives, tho' hard they be,
For love has made their labours light,
    O bring them back from wind and sea!

For whom shall we make fair the board,
    Or sweep the room, or light the fire,
If they should sink into the deep,
    Submissive to the sea's mad ire?
Here aged mother, sweetheart, wife,
    And children who scarce understand,
Kneel down and ask with tear and sob
    And heaving sighs, " Bring them to land."

The sky was fair when out they sailed,
    We let them go without the clasp
We might have given them had we thought
    That they would meet Death's awful grasp;
But now the threatening wind and wave
    Awake our souls in prayer to Thee.
O God, extend Thy saving grace
    To those in peril on the sea.

THREE.

We two were friends—two women, who just met
    And loved, and kissed each other, and were glad,
And walked for years along a common way,
    When skies were blue, when rains fell grey and sad,
Until he came, and laughing stood between;
    Then bit by bit her life from mine she drew,
Gently and slowly, so as not to hurt,
    And when she went away I scarcely knew.

Love came the first, the old primeval claim,
    The call from misty ages, clear and strong,
That will not be denied or hushed to sleep;
    Yet oft the days are wearisome and long.
She does not call or write; still, love is here,
    But, oh! why did she take her life from mine?
A voice within me mourns for my lost friend,
    Despite love's kisses, warm and rich as wine.

Did she, too love him? Oh, why were we three,
    Or being two why can't I let her go,
And feel the conqueror who has won the game?
    I never guessed that I should hurt her so.
It seems but yesterday we crossed the fields
    Wet with the morning dew; alone were we,
Arm linked in arm—and then a shadow fell
    Close to our feet, and sudden we were three.

Shall we be friends again, sometime, somewhere?
    After she sleeps the pain and grief away,
And meets me with the same old happy smile,
    The frank, free look she wore but yesterday?
Will she forget that sometime in the past
    A shadow came between, and she was one—
A weary shape between the earth and sky
    Who journeyed to a bed of dust—alone?

Howe'er it be, those years were not in vain;
    Those years when she and I were all in all,
And loved each other so, and cheered, and helped,
    Till from the ages came that restless call.
It must be she will come to me again,
    When passion dead is mouldering into dust,
And we shall be just two whose meeting eyes
    Remember only love, and help, and trust.

A RIDING SONG.

Oh, away, Oh away! Over hill-tops, and down
Through the still, purple valleys, away from the town!
Away from the shops, and the policemen, and lamps,
From the rich folk with swagger, and down-at-heel tramps.

Oh, away, and away, oh, my gallant, brown mare;
Both at table and stable a place will be bare!
I could stand them no longer, but stole right away
For a gallop with thee at the close of the day.

There's a dude who will yawn in the drawing-room soon!
Whilst we ride glad and free 'neath the light of the moon.
And my father will curse as he chews his moustache—
Oh the wild, little breeze shaking yonder red ash!

And my mother will tremble, poor dear, at his frown,
For she ever looks up as my father looks down,
But the man whom I love I'll look straight in the face.
Oh, away, bonnie Bess, was there ere such a race?

Oh, away and away! If each woman, like me,
Learnt to ride such a ride, all the world would be free!
And their forms would be straight as the look in their eyes,
And no coward be bred underneath the wide skies.

BEHIND THE MASK.

Behind this quiet smiling mask I moan
    " When shall I dare to be myself, O God!
And all my strength and all my weakness own,
    And my tired feet with Freedom's joy be shod? "
They never guess, who see me day by day,
    The loathing and the longing buried deep;
They read not the fine smile that oft doth play
    Around my mouth—nor guess how much I weep,
Weep inwardly, with tears that leave no trace!
    Not strong enough, O God, to break the chain,
Nor weak enough, content within my place
    To love the empty peace, the barren pain.
I hate the senseless mirror on the wall,
    The chat of ribbons, and the latest news
Of who is dead, and who in love doth fall;
    The price of butter, and the style of shoes!
What is it that I pine for? I scarce know,
    But something bigger, broader than a tomb,
For glorious winds, and piles of waist-high snow,
    For risks to run, for life, for gain, for doom!
To be some strong man's comrade—but instead
    My husband, like a woman, fears the wind.
Between the being born and being dead
    Life is an utter blank—a desert blind.
Within my room a little picture hangs,
    Of rugged hills that strive to touch the cloud,
A flaming bush there is of golden broom,
    Lit by the moon, who tears her misty shroud;
And down the narrow path a horseman rides
    And sends the pebbles rolling down the track,
And through the fearsome glen a brown stream glides;
    But craggy hills are towering at his back!
The home is for the woman, so they say;
    The seat within the crowded car they give;
And for the selfsame work the lesser pay,
    And when we err the harder task to live.
Where are your fallen men? They, shameless, pass
    Respected, honoured, welcomed. Women take
Their tainted lives—look up to them, alas!
    The foolish woman's heart in vain may break
For one to whisper " Never mind the past!
    All that is done and over. Start again!

Love loves through all things. Never heed the blast
    From this chill world—dear heart, I see no stain! "
What is it that I ask? A vaster work
    Than washing dirty dishes, thankless task!
Than making clean again the daily murk
    That covers senseless things, that's what I ask.
For space, for air, for hardships, and a chance
    To win the common wreath they toss to men;
For feet to climb, as well as follow, dance,
    And if I fall the hope to rise again.

PARTED.

He broke the promises he made;
He said "To honour,"—"To degrade,'
He should have said to say it true,
There was but fennel left, and rue!

Some women might have loved him still,
And closely clung through days of ill,
Still nursing hopes, each one more faint,—
I was a woman, not a saint!

When nature made this soul of mine
She made clear justice there to shine,
I can but love where I can trust—
I cannot kiss when trailed through dust.

I should have stayed, old women said;
Waited at night, and shared his bed!
Till children's eyes had searched my face
And read its hate, its scorn, disgrace!

He was a stranger in my sight,
When trust had flown—then flew delight
I did not scold, nor weep—I went
Unto a life as hard as Lent.

I loved the little house we had;
The fire, the pictures gay and sad;
The bright canary's joyous trill—
But loved it not above all ill.

I took a bare and cheerless room
That scarce was wider than a tomb,
And got up early, came home late,
As lone as bird without a mate.

But this was better than to stay
His bread to bite from day to day;
My shoulders, not my soul bowed down—
They said that it was strange in town!

And other men as I went by
Smiled meaningly into my eye,
And one smiled not, but pleaded well,
But still I walked alone through hell.

Is there no choice, no choice but this:
The libertine's, the drunkard's kiss
Or loneliness without an end;
The shoulders or the soul to bend?

And are they weak, or strong, who bear
The degradation—festering care,
Without a sigh till they grow old?
No; they are weak—'tis I am bold.

Homeless and friendless I went forth
Whilst cruel glances searched my worth,
But they—they fear the dark unknown
Which I have travelled all alone.

I made it better for some wife;
Patience becomes a poisoned knife
That cuts the throat of Progress grand,
And lets its rich blood rot the land.

I was at least a pioneer,
Against the jest, the laugh, the sneer,
I walked unflinching—I have shown
A woman weak can stand alone.

THE TONGUE.

God made the woman's arm soft, warm and white,
    And pencilled it with veins of harebell blue,
That it might cling to man with sweet delight,
    And clinging lead him better than he knew.
Then, looking on His work, God quickly thought
    That man's more powerful limb would foster wrong;
So on a crimson thread the force He wrought
    By which the woman wields her dreaded tongue.

BETRAYED.

Beware, ye flowers that open to the sun,
    He'll look into your hearts with flaming eye,
And tell the whispering winds what he has done,
    And they will laugh and tell it to the sky
Till God Himself shall hear, and, frowning, chide.
    Only to think, a summer's space ago
I did not fear the world so strong and wide,
    Yet now a little hamlet bends me low,
And sinks my proud head to the very dust,
    And it was love that brought me unto this,
A kiss too many, and the virtue trust,
    A pleading voice that begged and promised bliss.
Shut tight, ye little buds upon the tree,
    And do not heed the voice of sun and wind,
Or they will serve you as my love served me—
    Will slay you with a whisper, low and kind.
Christ loved too much, and so they drained His blood!
    O, let the rain like cataracts from the sky
Pour down and wash away that little wood,
    That in its soft, green grass no more may lie
Another lover with his magic tongue
    Which makes the truth a lie, a lie the truth,
Who shares with one the sunshine and the song,
    But leaves her in the days of storm and ruth!
And strew within my grave no blushing flowers,
    Confessing kisses given by the sun,
Or I shall wake and weep through endless hours—
    And lay me where no maiden's feet may run,
Lest I should murmur from my bed of dust
    A tale, to rob her heart of love and trust.

THE MOTHER.

I buy greatest joy with my tears,
    And I wear in my bosom a flower
To be withered, or spared to the years;
    And I learn for the first time my power!
For I stand face to face with old Death
    And I beat him away with my prayers,
And he spareth my little flower's breath
    At the brunt of my fiery despairs.

I sit in my small silent room
    Whilst the roses are blowing outside,
And my heart is a garden of bloom,
    For my one little flower has not died!
And the heather is blue on the moors,
    And the days are all golden and long,
Whilst I sit calm and happy indoors,
    With my heart full of motherhood-song.

I toil through the day, strong with love,
    And the night is sweet-parted in two
By a cry like a bird's in the grove
    As a pale morning comes, faint with dew.
And I ask not the gown rustling loud,
    Nor the ease, nor the gayness, nor rest,
For I wear robes of motherhood proud
    Through the bird and the flower at my breast.

THE VALLEY OF DREAMS.

Have you walked in the Valley of Dreamland,
    Where the shadows hang scented and deep,
Have you gathered its red and white roses,
    Laid your head on its mosses to sleep?
Once I roamed through its velvety hollows,
    But there came a fierce angel named Pain,
And she drove me with sword from the garden
    Where I never may wander again.

Have you walked in the Valley of Dreamland,
    With its soft sky of languishing blue?
O, you dream in that wonderful valley
    That each heart in the wide world beats true.
Then you wake with a start from your slumber,
    With the angel stern-eyed leaning o'er;
With the valley of dreams left behind you,
    And reality stretching before.

Have you walked in the Valley of Dreamland?
    Then whatever may come you are glad;
For the fragrance that hung round the roses
    Faintly floats when the journey grows sad.
When the hot sun burns fiercely upon you,
    You can catch the cool chime of its streams,
And your hot cheek remembers sweet mosses
    In the beautiful valley of dreams.

IF.

What would I do if I were a man,
With a lordly breadth of mental span,
    And the heart of a man in me?
Oh, listen well, and I'll answer well,
Or as well as the tongue of a woman may tell!
    First, I'd sail in a ship on the sea.

I'd call my ship by a maiden's name
As wild as a gull, pure, bright as flame,
    And put forth on the wide, salt sea!
And the mast might bend and billows roar,
I would plough every ocean and touch every shore
    Ere I turned my face homewards again.

I'd smoke a pipe with a big, black bowl,
And fear to lose it as 'twere my soul,
    Because of the one who gave it!
If one night it fell in roaring sea,
With the heart of a man fixed so firm within me,
    Should I not bravely plunge in to save it?

But, no, I'd not be that kind of man!
I'd boast me a breadth of mental span,
    And curse me, and buy another:
I would tell my love the pipe sucked well,
O, better than tongue of an angel could tell,
    And remorse in the next puff smother.

I'd watch the Trinidad cocoa-dance!
I'd chat with Brittany girls of France,
    My old black substitute burning;
My soul, clean, true to her who gave
The lost pipe that somewhere bobbed up on the wave,
    As the needle to pole-star turning.

But if I found, when I came at last,
With presents and sea-yarns of white squalls past,
    She'd married a low land-blubber,
I'd just smoke my pipe of old black bowl,
Which replaced the one lost though 'twas loved like my soul;
    Laugh, or curse, maybe, but no blubber!

But I'm just a girl in the window-seat,
Who sits and looks on the still, grey street,
    Whilst turning heel of a stocking!
With my soul away on the flashing spray,
That is golden by night, that is silver by day,
    Where the jolly, brave ships are rocking.

If ever a boy be born of me,
I'll sing him songs of hills and the sea,
    And he shall go far a-roaming;
Though I sit and sigh in window-seat
To catch, o'er the stones of the little grey street,
    The sound of his steps slow-coming.

THE CHILDLESS HOUSE.

Pathetically neat and clean, it seems to wait a guest!
  There is no movement on the hearth, no laughter on the stair,
No stir of life that makes more sweet the eventide of rest,
  No wee hand dims the windowpane—the hearth is always fair.
What mean the sphinxes black that crouch each side the hearth
    all day?
  At night they look like demons in the fire-light's changing glow;
Like demons who are whispering one long, sardonic " Nay,"
  As crouch they ready as to spring besides our hearth of snow.
Now solemn marks the dark, old clock the moments, minutes,
    years,
  And seems a big, black coffin-shape, with voice of awful doom.
The kettle joins the chorus like a voice that sings through tears,
  Whilst like a glittering snake the light darts o'er the still neat
    room.
O mystery of the gleaming fire that dies and has new birth,
  Once buried deep beneath the earth—a grand, primeval wood,
What mean the sphinxes black that haunt the desert of this
    hearth?
  They look so evil to behold 'tis hard to think they're good.
Thou fire that once was buried dark, and once was flashing green,
  Breaking with Springtime into bloom, with nests amongst thy
    leaves,
With lovers walking 'neath thy boughs of thick and glossy sheen,
  What means the mournful, ancient clock, with voice that
    endless grieves?
Our love sprang up like flame from dark of ages gone before,
  It had not grown in one brief life to be so fair a thing,
It must have passed a hundred times from death to life's bright
    door!
  We bought the house to front the sun and a sweet bird to sing.
And bright indeed my needles shone within the velvet case!
  O magic, ancient needle, thou hast worked the sails of ships,
As man went sailing, sailing from the well-loved woman face,
  Whilst she stayed in her chamber with the sigh upon her lips.
I told my shining needles they should do more glorious things,
  I promised I would thread them with bright blue, and gold and
    red,
For flow'rs on finest garments, whiter than an angel's wings,
  The fairest, sweetest garments that on grass were ever spread!
The frowning portraits on the wall look on me with disdain,
  As once bright needles crumble with the rust within their case;

231

I fear them in the gloaming or when skies are dark with rain,
  There's such a scowl of hate and scorn on every pictured face.
O fire that hid for ages long within the dark, old earth,
  Thou soul of ancient forest trees that fell so long ago,
What mean the sphinxes black that crouch on each side of our
  hearth?
  And what is that they mutter as thy light is dying low?

I shut my heart against the child whose laughter thrills the street,
  I shut my gate, and go within, my heart grown like a stone,
But over it both night and day there echo childish feet;
  Our house is dark though looking south, and love grows tired
  and lone.

LITTLE THINGS.

She was just a little singer,
    One whose name scarce further went
Than upon the air might linger
    The wood-vi'let's sweet, shy scent.

Not a critic carped or flattered,
    Told her weakness or her might,
For her dreams were never scattered
    Further than her hearth-stone white.

All their elfin, witching glory
    Poured forth by the firelight red,
As the children begged a story
    Ere they climbed the stairs to bed.

There are golden throats and glorious
    Flinging many a magic strain
To the raptured world, victorious
    O'er the seas of chance and pain.

But some bless the little singers
    With their humble coats of brown,
Chirping when the first beam lingers,
    Waking up the tired, grey town.

There are mighty, towering mountains,
    With proud crest of Alpine snow;
There are wondrous, irised fountains,
    Bowered where thund'ring cataracts go,

That are loved, but not more truly
    Then some tiny, nameless hill:
Heaven for some may bend more bluely
    O'er a tinkling, flower-veiled rill.

For the gods of peak and valley
    Fashioning a flower-cup sweet,
Thought of strength that could not rally,
    And made ways for little feet.

THE MANIAC.

Yes, they say I am mad, but I know
That my mind is as clear as the dew,
When it hangs on the bonnie, sweet briar
With the sun, moon and stars shining through.
And I love the good sun—he is warm!
And the bright stars will do me no harm;
But my heart sings a gay little tune
As I view through the window the moon.

Once the moon made me sad. Ah, but now,
As she rises my spirit is gay.
Once I wept, and the people seemed strange,
For they watched me, and whispered all day.
I will love the white moon to the end;
In that sad time she was my one friend,
For we used to walk by the sad sea,
And she sang sweet, sad stories to me.

Once I had a braw lover, so strong!
And as brown as a fall leaf was he,
As he sailed in a ship with red sail,
And they said he was drowned in the sea!
But the moon and I know, oh, we know,
For we went out when mad winds sunk low,
And the billows were murmuring a rune;
In a pool he slept, bright with the moon.

In a tide-pool he slept, of pale green;
And his face was not brown, yet 'twas he!
And a white star beside him had stayed;
He looked strange, but could not deceive me.
For the moon and I knew, wondrous wise,
That he slept, calm and safe, 'neath the skies;
So I oft stole away to the sea,
And I talked to the moon—she to me.

I was sad when the bright moon went home,
Leaving me with those people so wild;
They who chid me for laughter or tears,
Just as if I was only a child!
O, I laughed when she came back once more,
And we went for a walk by the shore,
Till we came to the pool. He was gone!
In the world I had no friend but one!

And my heart burnt within me like coal,
They had wakened him up as he slept,
In the pool with its bonnie, white star!
And my heart grew not cool though I wept.
Yes, they say I am mad, but I know
I'm but sad when the tide has gone low,
When the billows like tired babies cry—
Oh, how weary they murmur and sigh!

Who, ah, who, could have wakened my love?
And have stolen the star as he dreamed?
Who but people who said he was drowned?
Cried the wiseacre moon as she beamed.
And I knew one was he, his false friend,
Who would help me the torn nets to mend,
Though I told him I hated him deep,
Deeper far than a drowned man can sleep.

For he stole a sweet kiss that was his
Who sailed forth in the ship with red sail;
And the man who will kiss angry lips
Would awaken a sleeper so pale.
So I grasped close a knife my love gave,
And I silently walked by the wave,
And I waited until the thief came,
Then the knife bit his heart like a flame!

And I knelt down and hearkened him moan,
And he said, " God has great justice done,
For 'twas I sank the ship that he sailed
In the deep, from the beautiful sun.
Christ, forgive me! But Christ never knew
How the love in a human heart grew,
Nor how bitter a draught man must taste
His beloved by another embraced! "

Then I said " I will hate you in hell!
In your agony laugh at my own!
For you stole the white star from his pool;
Whilst he slept, full of trust, all alone!
Tell me, where is the kiss and the star?
Oh, I know they are hid, near or far! "
Then he moaned, " Oh, my sin! She is mad! '
And the moon and I laughed, precious glad.

Then his face grew as pale as the surf;
There was only the billow's low sigh;
And behold in the pool of my love
Fell the silver star down from the sky.
But the lost kiss he never gave back,
For in death was his soul stormy black—
But his groans rose no more by the sea,
And the moon and I laughed merrily!

Once I had a braw lover, so strong,
And as brown as a fall leaf was he,
As he sailed in his ship with red sail—
And they said he was drowned in the sea!
But the moon and I know, oh, we know,
For we went out when mad winds sunk low,
And the billows were murmuring a rune;
In a pool he slept, bright with the moon.

But I never could find him again,
Though I searched every pool—after this—
And I knew he had wandered away
Vexed with me for his false friend's base kiss.
And I sighed " Oh, forgive me, my friend,
As I sat down the torn nets to mend,
Looking out for your ship from the south,
Came your rival and wild-kissed my mouth.

" But you need not to think him I loved,
For, my friend, if you look on the shore,
He is killed with the knife that you gave—
He will kiss me, sweet friend, never more!
I come back and he down in the pool,
There's not one that's so pretty and cool;
And all day whilst the sad billows break
will sit there and sing till you wake."

And I might him have found (I don't know),
But they came and close fastened my hands;
" She is mad," was the tale that went round,
And the waves echoed " mad " from their strands.
There was only the moon faithful then
As I passed from the dwellings of men;
For they all were afraid of me soon!
And my prison knew but the pale moon.

Farewell, ships by the side of the sea!
Drown not men who are trusting to you!
Oh, I once watched a ship sail away
Through the dusk of a summer night's blue;
And my kerchief I waved till from sight
Went the ship with my whole life's delight,
And I thought " He will soon come again;
Oh, God guard him through wind and through rain."

I am now far away from the sea—
There's the shadow of trees on the floor,
And the wind in the branches at night
Seems the sea, with its pitiless roar.
Then I shriek " Drown the wild men who sail!
For why do they go out in the gale?
Splinter ships, Sea, and bury them deep,
And thus teach every woman to weep."

Then they take me away from the wind;
Where the moon cannot talk through the pane;
In a little dark room that is hot—
With their cruel hands on me again.
And I cry " Oh, my lover was kind,
Though his strength was the strength of the wind—
If you hurt me he'll know of it, soon
In his pool that is lit by the moon."

But I smother and sigh in that room,
With its one window far from the floor,
Where my lover could never look in,
(As he might) if he came from the shore.
And I beat with fierce hands the soft walls,
And I hear a wild voice that mad calls,
Till I find it is mine and I swoon,
And am woke up again by the moon.

As I sit on the floor in the sun
And I hold to my ear a sweet shell,
I can hear the sea boil round the boats,
And by rocks that are blacker than hell.
Thus I sit with my shell, and I dream
Of the wild petrel's joy-maddened scream
O'er the beach of a salt-scented town,
Till the sun red as blood has gone down.

And I once felt so happy and good,
And my brow grew so tranquil and cool,
Just as long, long ago, when a child
As I laved my hot hands in a pool.
So they took me outside to the wind,
And it kissed all my face, oh, so kind!
And I felt calm, and longing for sleep;
Far too happy to laugh or to weep.

But one day came a woman quite strange,
As her garments were black, just as white
Was her face—and she looked at me long,
And she made my good soul sick with fright.
For she looked like the face by the star,
Only wearier, sadder by far.
" Don't you know me? Remember my lad? "—
And I said " They will think you are mad.

" They will think you are mad if you cry;
If you laugh with a joy that is deep;
And the people who talk to the moon
Are all mad, and they love these to keep
Far away from the ones who are calm,
And whose words are not wild, but like balm,
But the folk who live here oft are gay—
Gayer far than those not shut away.

"It is only sometimes in the night
Awful forms come and taunt by your bed,
And they strike lurid lights on their thumbs,
Whilst their looks are more wan than the
dead.In their hands without flesh are red knives
That have cut throats of babes and of wives,
And you'd best be in dullest of holes
Than have visits from murderers' souls."

Then she turned and fled, and I felt glad
That she went ere the grim man came back,
He who thinks you are only a dog—
But I oft wondered why she wore black.
I hate black rocks, and trees, and black clothes;
I like white moons and stars—the white rose,
I would love a white house by the sea,
And I dream there is one built for me.

But I know what I'll do, yes, some-day,
I will leap, when there's no one to see,
From the window and leave this hard house,
Where they watch you and watch—I'll be free!
And the moon will lead me by the road
Till my heart and my brain lose their load,
And I come to my dear lover's pool
To find rest in its waters so cool.
O thou Moon!

A SINGER.

I am no beauty;
O beauty's a flower
That men's lips praise for a passing hour;
The closer they press it
The sooner it dies,
Then they toss it away
With light laughter—or sighs—
But what matter these to the flower that low lies?

I sing my songs,
I sing, O I sing,
Of Life and Death, of Love and of Spring!
All my beauty and power
In little, round throat,
As I rule vast crowds
With one rich, golden note—
With miserly longing upon it they gloat.

O what is a queen?
Let History tell
How her fame is bought by Misery's Hell.
The brighter it gloweth
'Tis fed by most fears
Sprung deep from the heart;
And the hot, thirsty years
Drink it like fierce suns—as if dew, and not tears.

But a singer's power
Resembles a bird's,
For were I to sing without sweet words,
The strong man would tremble
With bitterest grief,
His mighty heart stirred
Like a light aspen leaf—
Then quiver again with a joyful relief.

I had a lover,
Was it yesterday?
I only know I sent him away,
For I felt the glory
So keen and so strong,
Of the lark in the sky,
So it could not be wrong,
And I hope I may die ere I lose my song.

I love the cities
All gray with soft mist,
The weary faces tired and unkissed,
The glittering lamp-lights
Like big yellow stars,
The ride through the dusk—
And the orchestra's bars—
What joy strikes my soul with those preluding bars!

I love the perfume
Of flowers on my breast—
The faint, dainty jasmine I love best.
I love worn hands clapping,
But come with a start
From my throne in the sky—
But my song in their heart,
Shall remain and help heal the fever and smart.

And when I am old,
And weary and pale,
And my voice is a ghost so weak and frail,
I shall give them rapture,
O, yes, even then,
It still shall ring sweet
Through the great hearts of men,
Like the far, haunting echoes of evening glen!

For those who listened
    In life's brightest glow,
Will weep for beautiful things that go,
    For youth, with its yearnings,
    And magical gleams,
    That glisten no more
    Over Life's slower streams—
But have gone, like my voice, to places of dreams.

    But those who never
    Have heard it before
Shall muse what it was in days of yore,
    And nigh hush their heart-beats
    To catch every note,
    Like a swan's song sweet,
    From the thin, wrinkled throat—
The last note is God's—into silence to float!

THE HIGHLAND PIPER IN LONDON.

Fly, Piper, to the hills again!
Pipe not that weird majestic strain
'Midst city streets—poor hearts to shake
With longing dreams of fall and lake
In haunted glens where Silence sleeps,
For dark moors where the wild hare leaps;
Thy pipes unto the hills belong.
Degrade not so thy noble song.

Those pipes in freedom's fight have skirled,
Oh, sell them not unto the world;
Those same wild pipes that rogue, Rob Roy,
In firelit cave would greet with joy!
Let misty mountains, rock and scar,
Reverberate from near and far,
And red, red rowans sway and sigh
To hear the echoes melt and die.

Ah sordid, sad it seems to me
When mountains sell their melody;
That pipes which peeled through Hieland glen
Unto the tramp of rebel men
Should sound their songs for careless ear,
To rouse the smile, the stare and sneer—
Or—in the heart of Nature's child
Breed hopeless longings, fierce and wild.

244

A LAMENT.

I saw a woman lying in her grave,
Her yellow hair all dabbled in her blood,
Her little hands clenched close in agony,
Her lovely eyes in horror looking up
Through clay and water and the roots of weeds,
Her little mouth agasp to call for aid.
And as I looked upon her, dumb and blind
To all things else, she moaned, and moaning cried
" I went to meet my lover in the wood,
The little laughing wood of beechen green
Through which the convent-bell rung evening in,
And as I went I hummed a little song
That he had taught me on the wide sea-shore,
And danced a measure from the carnival,
And all the world seemed gay with life and love.
Ah, me! And I had thought he loved me well!
I went to meet my lover in the wood,
And found a man who had his looks and voice,
Who gripped me till my very heart was crushed,
Who would not hear my voice, but took his will,
His cruel tiger's will—and then, afraid,
Looked shuddering round upon the evening wood,
And murdered me. And yet I could not speak,
And could not say to him ' I love you well,
Though you dishonoured, and are murdering me!
Though you have never loved me, yet I love,
And pity you who feared me and did slay,
Who loved yourself, and hated when 'twas done.
O love is kind and lets itself go by,
But passion slays us in the name of love,
And hides in shuddering even from itself;
But if your hands had only loosed awhile
I could have said, " I love you, though you kill!"
I see them, see them, from my little grave
Hunting you down from town to city street,
In country wastes and o'er the barren heaths,
Where gipsy fires burn blackness yet more bare,
And I can nothing do to hide your tracks
For you have lain me helpless in my grave.
How cold a bed is this upon the clay
And dark without a candle's single gleam!
And here I lie, because you were afraid,

A coward following up a tyrant's rage.
Alas, dear love, that this should come from you,
And not from any wandering vagrant man,
Because I know, laid in the silence here,
That you have never loved me as you said,
For love would slay itself, not what it loved.
Gives honour, life, not death and shame.
Ah me!
I went to meet my lover in the wood,
And found he did not love me—but himself."

THE WOMAN IN THE DARK.

I heard a woman singing in the dark,
So sad and wild I could not choose but hark,
And in between her lines the restless sea
Sobbed weary anguish, roaming restlessly.

" O bitter, bitter when we crown a king,
And raise aloft a god with fine, strong wing,
And lowly place our heads beneath his foot,
And give him of our heart; yea, all its root,
And stand him in the naked light of day,
And midst the night's pure stars, a rod to sway
In one strong hand—the other clasps our world,
A jewelled pennon round about him furled,
Made of the tears of all our woman's pride,
Of all the thoughts of self we tossed aside.
O bitter, bitter when the gold turns black,
And all the stars of night mock at his back."

I heard a woman singing as I passed,
Far out at sea down dropped a splintered mast
And guns were booming, bellowing grief and pain,
And all the ragged coast was wrapped in rain.

"O bitter, bitter when our god falls down,
And our own hands must rob him of his crown,
And strip the gilded majesty away
To mocking laughter and the light of day,
And feel the broken rod run sharp as steel
Swift through the bleeding heart that still can feel,
And see the globe he clutched drop into dust,
And all the tears we gave turn into rust,
Yea, blood-red drops of rust no longer fair,
The pennon dropping down to leave him bare.
O bitter, bitter when we call his name,
And try our best to worship just the same."

Soft as the sobbing in the sombre pines
Majestic broodings muttered through her lines,
And through the darkness came a bird of white
And killed itself against the lighthouse light.

" O bitter, bitter when he does not know
That in the dust his head is lying low,
And still in voice imperial doth demand
The worship of the eye, the heart, the hand;
When none know that our god has tumbled down,
But only we behold him without crown,
When all acclaim and only we accuse
And wail in the hushed dark our god to lose,
Yet when the crowd go by who cannot see,
Must shout our praise, and shout it joyfully.
O bitter, bitter when our upward look
Leaves all our soul a sullen, joyless brook
That never can find rest from pain and dree
Until it knows the clean, refreshing sea."

Far out at sea a weary ship aground
Crashed to its last long fall with thundering sound,
The waves closed o'er it chafing restlessly,
And hid it in the depths where no storms be.

Ingram Content Group UK Ltd.
Milton Keynes UK
UKHW021301060723
424670UK00022B/502

9 781849 212120